SONNY BOY!

SONNY BOY!

THE WORLD OF

Al Jolson

Barrie Anderton

JUPITER

First published in 1975 by
JUPITER BOOKS (LONDON) LIMITED
167 Hermitage Road, London N4.

SBN 904041 352

Set in 12/14pt Monotype Baskerville 169 by
The Lancashire Typesetting Company Limited, Bolton.
Printed and bound in Great Britain by
R. J. Acford Ltd, Chichester, Sussex

Contents

Preface and Acknowledgements

THE twenty-fifth anniversary of Al Jolson's death falls on 23 October 1975, and, although he became part of my life only just before his death, scarcely a day goes by without my catching his name. Mention is constantly being made of the places he played, the shows he starred in, the people he knew, the songs he sang, the songs he wrote or helped to write, the records he made, the records he broke – the plaudits are endless. Al Jolson became a legend in his own lifetime and, even today, the legend lives on. This book is a tribute to that man and that legend.

I should not have been able to make this tribute without the help of a great many people who deserve more than the brief glory of an inclusion on the acknowledgements page. It would also be difficult to give individual credit to all the sources of information on which I have leant so heavily. My special thanks go to Les Kaye for his untiring efforts in the compilation of this book, and for lending and making available his collection of sheet music and original programmes; to Grahame Riddell for his work of love, some of which forms the basis of the script; to the late Dave Jay/Wigransky for *Jolsonography*, the definitive encyclopedia of Jolson which I published in 1969, and from which are taken sources, photographs, illustrations and cast lists. My thanks also to the current, and defunct, press and magazine publishers and their writers whose articles are all unanimous in their praise of Al.

Lastly I have to thank Al Jolson himself, not simply for the endless pleasure he gave and still gives to those who love him, but also for the great legacy he has left us.

Of the literally thousands of hours of tape I own of Al, and the hundreds of thousands of newspaper articles I have on him as a subject, there are not a handful of bad ones. There are no criticisms at all of this great man's stagecraft or of his voice – how could there be – and, although his ego sometimes brought him disfavour and not everyone loved him, all agree that he was a unique personality. But great treasures are not easily portable; such a cornucopia poses insoluble editorial problems. Anyone who finds what seem to be gaps should see the sheer volume of material that Les Kaye and I have scanned and, regrettably, had to bypass for lack of space. It would also, no doubt, be your pleasure, as it was ours, to listen to the numerous tapes of celebrities discussing Al, and revealing a wealth of anecdote and opinion far beyond the compass of a single volume. The omissions are sad, but inevitable.

When we were discussing the book, my publisher suggested that I should 'open with something big'. Pondering the best ways of following this advice, I was led, time and again, to the same conclusion. I remembered that I was writing of a man whose life was told on film, not once but twice, and of whom Maurice Chevalier said, when I asked him who were his greats – 'Only one, Jolson of course'. Here then is a book that can only start as it means to go on – with Jolson. What bigger opening could a book have?

The World's Greatest Entertainer

AL JOLSON was, in his own words, the world's greatest entertainer – an opinion echoed in the ecstatic applause that greeted him everywhere he went. He was a man who conjured with his voice, casting a spell over every gathering and managing by some miracle of regeneration to give himself to people, heart and soul, night after night. All his life he carried on an unashamed love affair with his audience, an affair that lasted when everyone said that it was over because it was founded on love strong enough to survive one long separation and some serious rifts. When he died, Al Jolson was a household name, acknowledged by all the world to be prodigiously talented, fabulously rich and fervently American. However, in the best fairy-tale tradition, his beginnings were far removed in every way from his later life; for when he was born the World's Greatest Entertainer did not even own the name by which the world was to know him.

Asa Yoelson was born in 1885 or 1886 in Srednik, a small village then on the borders of Russia and Poland, and now part of Lithuania. He was the youngest of the four surviving children of Cantor and Mrs Moses Reuben Yoelson. His mother, Naomi, had lost her first child in its infancy, but Rose, Etta, Hirsch and finally Asa all survived to grow up in the atmosphere of strict Hebrew orthodoxy by which their family had lived for generations.

The Yoelsons were of good peasant stock, honest and hardworking, and for many generations at least one Yoelson had entered the church to become a cantor. Naturally it was one of the cherished hopes of Cantor Yoelson that one, if not both, of his sons would take the same road. Although he was to be disappointed, it must be said that, prior to following the dictates of family tradition and of his own heart, Moses Yoelson had nursed his own secular ambitions. He had thought seriously of becoming an opera singer and music always remained, after his faith, the guiding passion of his life. What this rigidly pious man really thought of his sons' careers is debatable, but the effects on the boys of the family's twin passions – music and religion – is indisputable; music was in the family's blood, practised, played and appreciated with religious fervour, and there is no doubt that it was upon the rock of their father's religious music that the two boys' more profane talents were built.

Because of their father's beliefs and position, life for the Yoelson family was strict and unremittingly subservient to the laws of the church. Each day the children attended the *chayder* (Hebrew school) for an hour and went to the synagogue three times. Nor were these excursions their only religious activities. Because of the many domestic rituals and ceremonies in the Hebrew faith, the children probably saw little distinction between the synagogue and the three rooms of their simple log-built home. Even when they played on the cottage's earthen floor, their simplest games and pastimes might be transformed into religious acts, as at the Feast of Maccabees when tops were spun, or during the reading of the story of Esther when rattles would sound at every mention of Haman's name.

Since religion influenced not only their spiritual development but the day-to-day conduct of their lives, it was entirely predictable that the cantor would begin to train the boys' voices almost as soon as they could talk. Equally predictably, no boys in the village knew the Sedar service like Hirsch and Asa. On the evenings of the Passover, the whole family would sit at table, their heads covered, and it became a regular occurrence for neighbours to peer in at the window to listen and watch. On such occasions the cantor would glance at his children, and smile.

There are some truths as old as any religion and far more universally acknowledged. One says that boys will be boys, and to this law Hirsch and Asa were no exception. Even under the vigilant eyes of their parents, they often became involved in the village fights that took place with other children. Sometimes, of course, they fought between themselves, and from an

Harry Jolson, Al's life-long mentor and support, is pictured here in happy mood as he appeared in *The Ghetto Sport*.

early age Asa would tear into his brother, who was three years his senior. But, with the village children, the two Yoelsons would always fight side by side, Hirsch doing his utmost to shield Asa – a habit in which Hirsch persisted throughout his life. To their parents, who had perhaps forgotten the complexities of childhood, all strife, domestic or civil, was Hirsch's fault. Asa's innate talent for going astray under his own steam, they completely overlooked.

Though the Yoelson children may have had their differences with the other village minors and the family's religiosity may have set them somewhat apart, all the villagers were united by their peasant status and their poverty. Life in the Russias at that time was one of extremes; families were either wealthy or poor, leisured or toiling. But, for all its inequitable harshness, the existence of these people had its compensations. It was simple and measured, and even though the Czar was cruel and oppressive, the people did not suffer the stresses of our modern existence.

The Yeolsons may have been poor, just like their neighbours, but they did occasionally manage to budget for leisure as well as necessity. One memorable summer, the cantor decided that it would be possible to take his family on a steamer to Kovno. This simple trip was like a journey to another planet. For days Naomi Yoelson made preparations for the journey and, at last, the moment came when Moses, Naomi, Rose, Etta, Hirsch and Asa all embarked for Kovno, a town of 50,000 inhabitants, with more enthusiasm than others might muster for a metropolis one hundred times the size. Careful as their mother was, on this special occasion, to watch over her brood, Asa was still able to stray from the fold. It was to the maligned Hirsch that the family's gratitude went for finding the youngest member of the family – and probably one of the few occasions when Hirsch was not held to be at fault.

More regular for the villagers than such excursions, and much less welcome – in the adults' eyes at least – were the annual incursions of the military. The children were delighted to have the soldiers amongst them, to watch their drilling and copy their movements. But the spectacle which enthralled the children was, for their parents, a command performance of a much more tiresome kind. Under the Czar it was decreed that each family would act as 'host' to these soldiers, without payment and without dissent. A few days prior to the main assault, an official representing the Czar would walk into each home, count the number of rooms and decide how many soldiers were to be 'entertained'. Argument was not encouraged. Naturally the allocation of individuals was as arbitrary as the numbers of them which were to be accommodated. Some of the 'guests' were rough and brutal, others were, like the Yoelsons, simple, homely Jewish peasants. These sympathetic lodgers often turned out to hate military service, which was compulsory.

Against this background of harsh government and enforced intrusions on the sanctity of his home, Moses Yoelson, like his illustrious namesake, came to the conclusion that it was time to move on. As the children of Israel had done in Egypt, so people in Russia began to look to a promised land, where, if the milk and honey did not exactly flow, at least newcomers were free to earn enough to buy them. Some in the village had already left their homes to journey to this latter-day Canaan, and many of those who remained behind, at the end of the long day, would sit in the twilight making their own plans for this long road to America. Of necessity, these plans were secretive and closely guarded. Bribery was the chief factor in forging the key that opened the gate to freedom.

Cantor and Mrs Yoelson were no exception to this general scheming. Uppermost in their thoughts was this dream. As the children got older and began to understand, they would often hear their parents discussing plans for departure, talking of the day when they in their turn would leave Srednik far behind.

Eventually, there came a night in the life of the Yoelsons that Hirsch was long to remember. The four children had been in their beds for some time when Hirsch felt on his shoulder the firm, gentle hand of his father. 'Hirsch,' said his father softly, 'while I am gone, you will take my place and will look after Mamma and the others. Each day you will attend the synagogue and *chayder*. Soon we shall be together again.' With these words and a long farewell look at his sleeping kin, the cantor left the room. Shortly afterwards Hirsch heard his father leave the house. The plans that had been so carefully laid were now being carried out. Moses Yoelson was on his way.

Four years were to elapse before the children saw their father again. After surmounting obstacles, anticipated and unforeseen, often having to travel disguised, Cantor Moses Reuben Yoelson finally arrived in New York, via Hamburg.

The year was 1890 and the first part of his dream had come true – he was in the U.S.A. The second part, that of his family joining him, had now to be realised. To put aside the necessary money, the cantor had to forego all but the essentials to keep body and soul together. The years from 1890 to 1894 must have seemed interminable, but the day did eventually dawn when he sent a letter to the family in Srednik bidding them come. In 1894, greeted like so many other immigrants by the unwavering salute of the Statue of Libery, Naomi Yoelson and her four children arrived in New York. For the American nation, the arrival of another batch of immigrants, among them a boy who would become one of its most famous adopted sons, was insignificant. For one new American, a family man who had lived alone for four years, it was one of the happiest days in his life.

When they met their father once more, Hirsch was twelve and Asa nine; during the cantor's four-year absence, their memory of him had become a trifle blurred. At first they did not recognise the figure standing on the quayside. Bewildered as the children must have been by a father they hardly knew any more, they must have been doubly confused by their speedy departure from New York. Within four hours of their arrival, they were on their way to Washington D.C., in the south-eastern part of which their new home was situated, close to the naval yard.

In the absence of the cantor, their religious training had been less strict but he was quick to set their feet on the path once more. Nevertheless, four years is a long time to be without the guidance of a father like the cantor and, to his dismay, he found his task increasingly difficult. Their drastic change of environment largely explained this intractibility; life in Srednik and life in Washington were very different. It took only a short time for Cantor Yoelson to realise that, not only would it be hard to steer his family along orthodox lines, but there would never be a Cantor Yoelson among his sons. This was a great blow to him.

Domestic problems apart, the four children were soon happily settled in the new surroundings and both parents saw their brood – especially the boys – change from European peasant children into sturdy young Americans. Picking up the language was no problem, and it was during these early and impressionable years that Asa began to talk with the pronounced southern accent common to many youngsters

Harry Jolson, looking younger than his 68 years but rather careworn, posed for this in 1951, the year after Al's death.

belonging to the east side. In contrast to his offspring's easy adoption of a new tongue, the cantor's English was always to remain slow and halting.

Their trouble-free settling was, however, marred by the illness of their mother. Never a strong woman, Naomi Yoelson had been through an exhausting time in the solitary

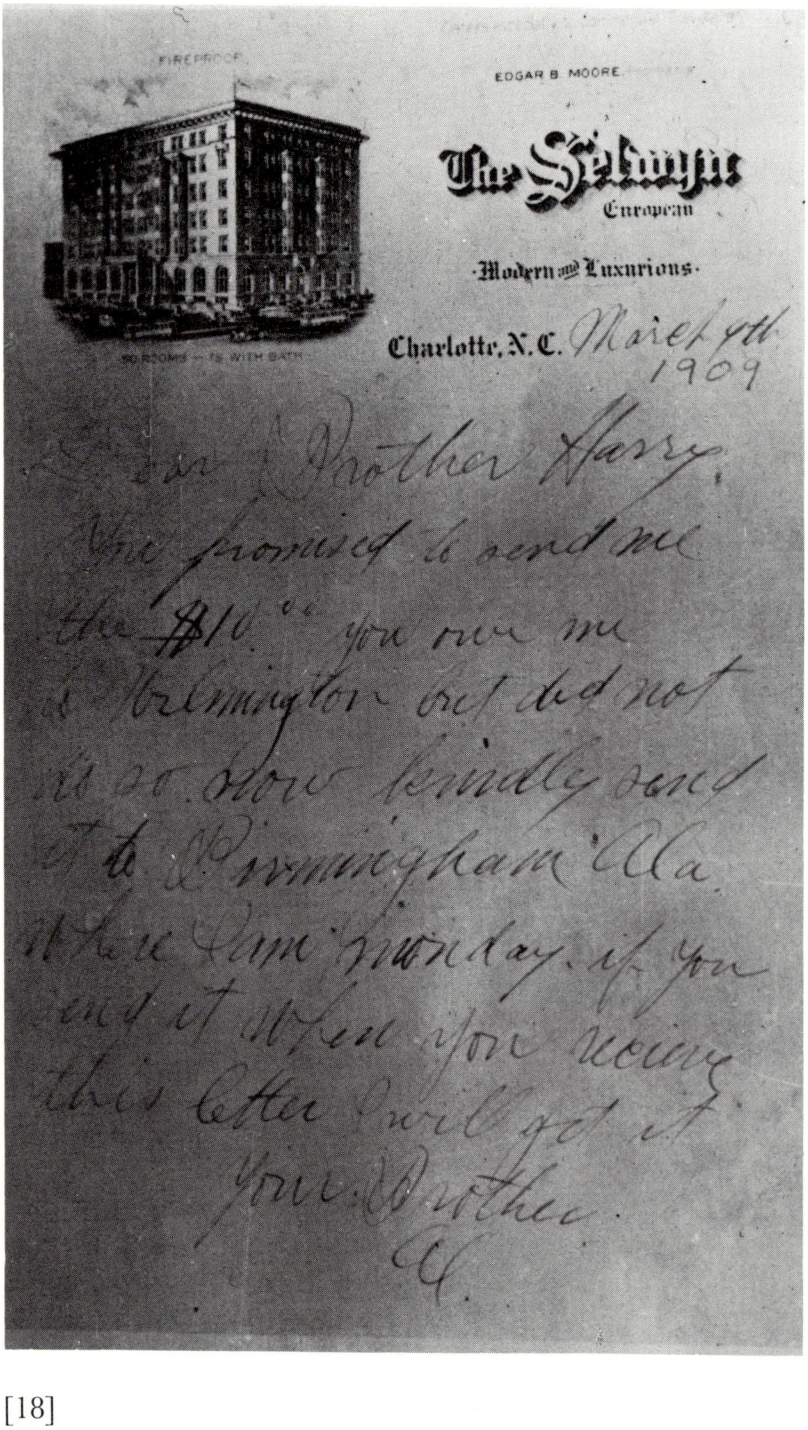

FIREPROOF

EDGAR B. MOORE

The Selwyn
European
·Modern and Luxurious·

Charlotte, N.C. March 9th 1909

Dear Brother Harry:
You promised to send me the $10.00 you owe me in Wilmington but did not do so. Now kindly send it to Birmingham Ala. where I am Monday. If you send it when you receive this letter I will get it.
Your Brother
Al

9 March 1909, as good a day for a little brotherly business as any. The contents of this letter – Harry owed Al $10 – should not make us forget that Harry was quite as successful as Al at this time.

years prior to the family's emigration. For those four years, she had looked after the children without the help of her husband, and this, together with the strain of the journey, had told on her. Soon after their arrival in Washington, her health began to decline rapidly, and she died during the winter of 1895.

A heavy sky threatened snow on the day that the benumbed family laid her to rest. Hirsch and Asa were without overcoats, on Asa's hands were old woollen stockings. Hunched against the cold and his bewildered grief, dabbing his makeshift mittens to his eyes, he made a brave effort to fight off the stinging tears, as they stood by the grave under that desolate winter canopy. In accordance with their faith, Kaddish – the prayer for the dead – was said for one year, but it was a day that was to linger many years longer in the minds of these simple people.

Following the death of Mrs Yoelson, Rose, the eldest, took charge of family affairs and became 'mother'. At this time, Hirsch was thirteen and Asa ten, old enough – they decided – to be wage earners and contribute to the family exchequer. The Yoelson brothers became newspaper boys and, at the end of the day, would count their earnings – a matter of cents – and proudly hand them to their sister. The newspaper boys led a rough and tumble existence and both learned the life of the urchin quickly. But, if their language and some of their habits betrayed this street schooling, their general behaviour showed that the lessons learned at home had not been forgotten. Stealing and other of the shabbier acts of urban living they firmly resisted.

About this time, the Yoelson boys fell prey to a new infatuation – the theatre. With the end of each day, after their contribution had been handed to Rose, anything that remained gained them admittance to this exciting and forbidden world. The cantor was horrified at his sons and feared for their morals. Selling newspapers was bad enough, but now, out of choice and not necessity, they were drinking at this certain source of corruption. His protests were in vain; his sons were entirely the slaves of their new passion. All he could do was to tax them with their weakness. 'Loafers!' he would shout, and it was many years before he was able to think of theatre folk in any other terms.

For Hirsch the time had come to leave the fold. As a useful supplement to their income from the newspapers, he and Asa

The beginning of the beginning for Al – Joe Palmer, who had a small, but well-established reputation, was the man who suggested that Al should perform in blackface.

would run any errands that came their way. Hirsch had helped a local politician in distress and had been rewarded handsomely with ten dollars. This king's ransom safely tucked in his pocket, he set off for New York with all the dauntless vigour of youth.

New York survived the shock of Hirsch Yoelson's arrival apparently without having noticed it, but his departure from Washington was not nearly so casually received. Asa was still at home, but reckoned that anything that Hirsch could do he could do as well. He too left for New York and that city, once again, affected not to notice the arrival of a Yoelson.

Within two hours of Asa arriving in New York he had found his way about that vast city, and had managed, amazingly enough, to find his elder brother. Asa's joy was unbounded but his brother may have been less ecstatic. For Hirsch it only meant added trouble. His ten dollars had gone, and both were now faced with the problems of eating and sleeping without a cent between them. Eating became the exception rather than the rule, and their sleeping quarters – park benches and empty rail wagons – were chosen for their discreet situation rather than their comfort.

Fifteen miles away, on the outskirts of New York, lived an uncle for whom their sister Etta kept house. It was on this sister that the two boys were eventually forced to call for assistance. Unfortunately, their welcome was neither open-armed nor open-handed; Hirsch was severely upbraided and given two dollars to see him on his way while the young Asa

Cantor Moses Reuben Yoelson, Al's father – strictly religious but also passionately interested in music, he unconsciously encouraged the two brothers in their eventual careers.

was packed off home. There he stayed for two weeks before running away again.

His return to New York was more auspicious, and he managed to land a bit part with, what was in his eyes, the illustrious Rich and Hoppe Company. For a twelve-year-old to whom the difference between the Palace and Rich and Hoppe was neither apparent nor important, it was an incomparable experience. His stay with the company was short-lived, but before returning to Washington, he attended the Bijou Theatre where he watched a blackface singer who was to achieve great success later as Eddie Leonard. Part of Eddie Leonard's act was to call upon the audience to join in with one of the choruses, a request that was never met – until this particular night. The bold Asa needed no encouragement, and with all the aplomb and experience of his twelve years, he gave forth, much to the pleasure of the audience and Eddie Leonard. Leonard immediately sought out the young nightingale and made him an offer, but the cantor intervened, and Asa remained at home.

Soon after this adventure, there arrived in Washington *The European Sensation*, a show starring Aggie Beeler. One of the most popular songs in the show, 'My Jersey Lily', was sung by Miss Beeler, with the same invitation to sing along that Eddie Leonard had made. Again Asa rose to the occasion, again the audience were delighted, again Asa was sought – and again the cantor refused to let his boy join the ranks of 'those loafers'. This time, however, he prohibited in vain. One morning shortly afterwards, Asa did not appear at breakfast.

So the trumpet of Asa's destiny had sounded, he had heard the call and followed. Meanwhile, the theatre had also called to Hirsch who had likewise heeded the invitation. The brothers Yoelson had finally entered the world of show business, though each was working independently of the other. Within a short space of time, Cantor Yoelson appeared to have lost two sons, and the theatre gained two young suitors. Harry and Al Jolson, born Hirsch and Asa Yoelson, were about to enter an estate more binding, more demanding and more rewarding, for one of them anyway, than marriage. Both were to find it a fruitful relationship, and for Al it was to grow into a love for which he lived and died.

However, as if to show that the break with their past was not complete, at the start of their chosen careers they were to

This picture of Al taken in 1900 recalls his first days in Washington when both Al and Harry sold newspapers to boost the family's income.

White

FEINBERG

call themselves Harry and Al Joelson. The first names had been quickly 'Americanized' to conform with fellow youngsters on the streets of Washington D.C. The name Yoelson had its 'Y' replaced by a 'J' when they presented themselves to teachers for what was to prove the most rudimentary of schooling: since the two brothers could barely write in the new tongue, the teachers recorded their name as it was pronounced to them.

The nineties were the years of the sentimental ballad, when the hearts and eyes of performer and audience alike were required to be brimming at all times. It was during this era, in 1897, that *The European Sensation* – with Al Joelson singing from the gallery – was on the road. Audiences had fallen in love with his fine treble voice, and he had fallen in love with audiences, experiencing that sweet emotion which, once savoured, he was to yearn for always. So life went on happily enough and Al's spirits soared as high as his captivating voice – until, one day, the pearl-pure voice began to break, and, with each fractured note and falling octave, down crashed all his hopes.

Voices are breaking and being remade in a different, yet equally fine mould all the time, but Al would not be persuaded of this and was inconsolable: he had left the show; he was out of work; and he would never sing again. His brother Harry, who was near at this time, did all he could to persuade Al that it was only a phase from which he would emerge unscathed. All arguments failed then and, indeed, at intervals during the whole course of his life, Al would be haunted by the thought of losing his voice completely. Perhaps his only consolation in this difficult period was that, beside his singing, he had also developed quite a breezy style as a whistler.

At the back of Harry's mind for some time had been the idea of a double act – the Joelson Brothers – and Al was enthusiastic once his voice was over the breaking stage. So it was that the Joelson Brothers act, 'The Hebrew and the Cadet' came into being. At the same time Al and Harry added another string to their bow. A form of entertainment very popular at the turn of the century, was the Singing Waiter. Usually at weekends, when business was brisk, proprietors of restaurants would engage entertainers who could also serve the customer. If the customers liked a particular entertainer, they would show it by throwing coins in his direction. Some of these restaurants were nothing more than 'joints' but even

The year is 1900 and the 14-year-old, seen here with Fred E. Moore, obviously has no doubts about whose century it is going to be.

entertainers had to eat. In this capacity the two brothers were able to get employment, at the same time acquiring songs, material and the facility for 'putting them over'. Many of the great entertainers commenced their careers in this way.

'The Hebrew and the Cadet' act was typical of its kind and, on reflection, rather corny, but in its day met with a certain measure of success. The part of the Hebrew was played by Harry and the Cadet by Al, and, although the act didn't play to capacity houses, at least it played. This was before the days of the welfare state and life was hard for a 'resting' artist. When the act didn't play, the act didn't eat. For the struggling brothers, breadwinning was to be only an intermittent occupation for some time.

Small-time entertainers would often imitate the style of the big names and copy their lines, often stealing them outright to present as their own. In fact Eddie Cantor related, many years after he had achieved fame, that in his early days he was unable to play the better circuits because all his material was lifted from well-known comedians of the time and he was without his own. Naturally, in the case of the great artists, this was only a passing phase – the 'growing pains' of the trade. The Jolsons, being human like everyone else, went through these growing pains.

It is doubtful whether anyone today will know the name of Joe Palmer. Yet, in his time, all who followed the stage were familiar with his fine baritone voice. His was an unfortunate case because he was stricken with a nervous complaint, for which there seemed to be no cure, and confined to a wheelchair. The fine voice still remained, but his incapacity placed certain restrictions upon him as a solo performer.

Friends of Harry and Al suggested teaming up with Joe Palmer to form a trio, and, as he was still known and would thereby provide a 'name', it seemed an excellent idea. Joe Palmer readily agreed. The act became known and billed as Jolson, Palmer and Jolson, so presenting the name by which the world knows Al, for the first time. The 'e' was dropped simply to make the billing shorter.

It was a good act. Until now, Al had always played straight parts and felt at ease in the various roles, but Palmer wished him to play comedy. Much against his own better judgement, Al gave way to his elder partners, and was an instant success. Regular bookings followed and the act, entitled aptly 'A Little of Everything', did well. Al's part in this was as the

Al looking unusually contemplative, in *Vera Violetta* (1911), his second show at the Winter Garden.

Al is seen here with Stella Mayhew in the Shubert Brothers' *La Belle Paree* (1911), his first show on Broadway.

bell-boy. It offered the audience a little comedy and a song, and was well received. Nevertheless the performers felt that the act lacked a certain 'something', and it was not until the three of them were playing at the Keeney Theatre in Brooklyn that they found the answer to this deficiency. There the actor-singer James Francis Dooley suggested to the team that, like himself, Al should try blackface. This paid immediate dividends, and so it was, in the year 1904, that Asa Yoelson, son of a Russian-Jewish cantor, completed the metamorphosis which made him Al Jolson, blackface singer and 'The World's Greatest Entertainer'.

It has often been asserted that Al Jolson was the first of the

Lew Dockstader, a great leader of troupes, gave Al his professional education when the Dockstader Company toured the length and breadth of the country.

brothers to appear in blackface. This was not the case; Hirsch anticipated him when he appeared in a burlesque show called *The Mayflowers*. Despite this, Hirsch was sometimes in later years accused of imitating his younger brother.

The Jolson-Palmer-Jolson combination did quite well together, but later became a double act of Palmer and Jolson, the Jolson part of the act being of course, the young Al. Harry had branched off on his own and was on the way to making quite a big name in the theatre. It was not until later that he came to feel that the shadow of his younger brother was keeping him in the cold.

Jolson and Palmer were never 'big time', but they did get regular bookings, and Al was gaining more and more experience. However, just as the threesome had been a stepping stone for Al, so the team of Palmer and Jolson was only a further stage. Eventually Palmer and Jolson parted, Joe Palmer to give up show business almost entirely, Al to perform on his own and work hard at developing his own style.

From the time he played with his brother and Joe Palmer in 'A Little of Everything', throughout the many years of performance, one thing was to remain – his blackface make-up. In fact it was not until *Wonder Bar* in 1931 that Al Jolson was seen in musical comedy with a white face.

Al, with his beautiful tenor voice and blackface, was an instant success, winning the hearts of the theatre-going public wherever he performed. It was perhaps in San Francisco that he was loved most of all, and so 'blindly' that many imagined he was a native of that place. Chicago, though, approached San Francisco in its ardour and, on one occasion, turned out almost all its citizenry and a police escort to welcome him. Tumultuous receptions in the streets were reserved for the future, however, and for the time Al was content to be well received in the theatres he played.

Now that he was on his own, Al was not only able to monopolise the applause, but he could also work on his style. He began to develop a style of singing all his own. Another thing that made his isolation splendid was that he did not have to divide the takings. He was by now earning seventy-five dollars a week, a sum that soon rose to $125, and he felt rich. The newspaper boy was getting ahead, but, unfortunately, did not acquire an increasing prudence along with this rising wage; he was not a saver at any time in his life. It was while Al was playing San Francisco that the manager

of the Wigwam Theatre, a certain Mr Harris, saw and liked his work. Harris was able to offer the singer $175 per week. To Al this was a veritable fortune. He was mindful of the old saying that opportunity knocks but once. He was also mindful that he was a young man – and decided to take no notice of the old saying. 'Mr Harris,' said the young Al, 'I'm sorry I can't take you up on your offer, but it ain't enough.'

Harris's answer Jolson never disclosed, but he did say that Harris almost threw him out of the office. It looked as though his gamble had not come off. However, a day or so later, the same Mr Harris got in touch with him and offered him the $250 for which Al had risked his professional skin. All his life Al Jolson was to take risks and Providence generally arranged that they paid off.

At this time, the sound of wedding bells was added to the other music in Al's life, and he married, as he put it, 'the nicest girl in the world'. Henrietta Keller was her name and Oakland was the town that was privileged with her birth. In the eyes of Al's father, Oakland's loss was not much of a gain for the family. Henrietta was a gentile, and the marriage provoked his sternest reproofs. To Al, the girl from Oakland was worth all the wrath his father could visit on them.

In Henrietta he had the perfect partner: she was gentle and kind, and did her very best to be worthy of the man she felt was destined for great things. She saw that he at least made some attempt to look after his money, disapproving strongly of the way he spent so recklessly. It was during one of her chiding sessions that he turned to her quietly and said, 'Money? Money? Why should I save money? Someday I'll be a millionaire – I shall be the world's greatest entertainer.' Henrietta tactfully said nothing, but was not to realise that this teasing, idle boast would later become a generally accepted statement of fact.

Just as Harris had seen Jolson and leapt at him, so another man was to see him at work and help him on the way. This time it was none other than the great Lew Dockstader, who at that time was on tour with his famous Minstrels. Al had been spotted in one of the vaudeville houses by Will Oakland, a famed counter-tenor in Dockstader's line-up, and he was so impressed that he rushed off to tell his boss about the youth. At Dockstader's invitation, Al Jolson joined this illustrious troupe and was allowed, in addition to taking his part in the traditional minstrel show, to do his own speciality act.

In this curious uniting of nations, Al stands between Clarence Harvey and Lawrence D'Orsay in *The Whirl of Society* (1912).

It is here that the Jolson story really starts. Until this time, he had been knocking round the country, touring it from end to end, gaining the kind of hard-won experience that was to stand him in good stead now that he had finally arrived. As always with him, Providence appeared to be looking after his interests, and he was seen and heard by people who recognised his talent and were in a position to help him exploit it. The year was 1908, and in February 1909 Al and the Dockstader troupe went to New York. He was a great success there and now, playing the big cities with a big company, began to sense just how far he could go. While he was in New York, Al enjoyed another stroke of luck. Harry, who was already well known to New Yorkers, was also playing in town, and the critics, who liked Al's work, spoke approvingly of him as the brother of Harry Jolson.

Although there is no doubt that Harry's good name helped pave the way for Al, it is also clear that, at this stage, one of the brothers should have changed his name. Though neither, of course, could tell how things were going to pan out, the complications of two successful figures working in the same field with the same name are obvious to us who have the advantage of hindsight. However, even with this advantage, it is difficult to see a satisfactory solution. To Harry, an entertainer firmly established in the eyes of his public, a change of name would have been professional suicide. To us, even if logic says that Al should have been the one to take an alias, it is unthinkable that there should be no Al Jolson. Whatever the merits of the case, they can only be discussed speculatively, since neither Harry nor Al made any recorded comment on the problems, if any, occasioned by their shared name.

Al may have been given an unwitting leg-up by Harry, but it was his regular appearance with Dockstader's famous team that really helped the singer's rapid climb. Al was able to acquire first-class experience and a poise that he would have otherwise learnt only slowly, if at all. He also had the benefit of competent and familiar accompaniment. Normal vaudeville artists had to contend with a different pit orchestra in every place they played. Singers were entirely at the mercy of the competence and sobriety of these orchestras, which could make or mar the whole performance. Of course, standards varied from the passable to the impossible, and when an orchestra was abysmal, it always took the singer down with it. With Dockstader it was different. He engaged a good band

Al does as the Venetians do in *Dancing Around*, which the Shubert Brothers presented at the Winter Gardens in 1914.

that toured with the troupe, and rehearsals were given whenever required. From the time Jolson joined the troupe, he was never to know any but the best bands.

By the third year of his period with Lew Dockstader, Al was the troupe's biggest crowd-puller, getting standing ovations wherever they played and even usurping the sacred closing spot from Dockstader himself! When the show had its 'resting' periods he would play the vaudeville houses as a single act with equal success. Al was grooming himself for the day – not far off now – when he would be crowned king of musical comedy.

At this point the Shuberts of Shuberts' Theatre took the Dockstader Minstrels over, and so Al's contract at once became the property of Jack Shubert. Up until now Al had been happy with the way his reputation was growing, particularly in New York, and with the overall course his career was taking. He was naturally apprehensive about any change in his life and wondered what the future under Shubert would hold for him. Shubert, for his part, was not agonising over Al or his future. He saw acts richly seamed with talent every day, how was he to know he was looking at the motherlode?

One morning in 1911, the new owners, all unaware, called upon their goldmine to appear for rehearsal in a new show entitled *La Belle Paree* or *A Jumble of Jollity*. The show – lavish, spectacular and with an excellent cast – duly opened on 20 March 1911 at the Winter Gardens. Al Jolson was just another entertainer on the bill, he had only a small part and, to further complicate matters, he also had competition in the shape of Stella Mayhew, a well-known female blackface performer. It is not certain that Stella Mayhew was the first female blackface performer to take her act from the vaudeville houses to the Broadway stage, but it is certain that Al Jolson was the first male to do this and dare to take on a negroid role different from the conventional 'black butler' type.

With Dockstader Al had been a success, but then he had been part of a well-tried and well-established troupe. His success was in some sense ready made. In contrast, the Shuberts' *La Belle Paree* was an unknown quantity, there was no Lew Dockstader to help and he was doing his own spot, albeit a small one, in a Broadway show. Al may have had more misgivings at this time than he had known for a long while.

'Mr Jolson is the highlight of the evening' if this photo of him in *Robinson Crusoe Jr* (1916, Winter Garden) is anything to go by.

The show turned out to be good, but, as was so often the case, too long. Many a good show foundered because there was overmuch of it, and the length was certainly crucial to those artists, like Al, who were to appear last on the bill. They would often face a fractious audience who had already seen enough or, worse, an emptying theatre. It was not the best time to go on a stage and Al knew it.

The singer's opening night was fair and the audience, those that remained, received him quite cordially. In his own view, however, he had flopped. The audience hadn't taken off the roof when he came on – so a flop he must be. Neither the thought nor the sight of failure is pretty and, as he reflected on his failure in his first big chance, it seemed to him that ruin must be staring him in the face. When the theatre closed on that opening night he could not bear to go home. Instead he walked the streets all night, eating his heart out. When he did finally return home in the early hours of the morning, he was met by a Henrietta beside herself with worry and quite convinced that something must have happened to him. His protestations that something had happened – something as bad as any of the disasters that her imagination had contrived for him – fell on deaf ears. As long as Al was home safe and sound, she didn't care if he never performed again.

The critics too took a more sensible view of his début than Al did, and one said this of him: 'Equally amusing was Al Jolson – whether he is Alfred or Albert this modest seceder from Vaudeville will not divulge – who possesses genuine Negro unction in his speech and manner. Yet, by race, he might be thought capable of succeeding with other types.' Whatever Al or the critics thought about his performance, Fate again conspired, this time with Jack Shubert, to help the singer out, and save him from the oblivion to which he had so hastily consigned himself. For the second performance, the show was cut and Al thus appeared earlier in the evening. Given a fair chance with his act, he was a success overnight. So it was that on 21 March 1911, Asa Yeolson presented his calling card to New York. It stated, quite clearly: 'Al Jolson has come to stay'. The future King of Broadway had arrived to claim his throne.

It took only a short time for him to become an established star and favourite. He signed a long-term contract with the Shuberts and played opposite such great names as Gaby Deslys in *Vera Violetta*, and the famous Jose Collins. Although

Al with Lawrence D'Orsay, Hazoll Cox and friend in Sinbad (1918), another Winter Garden extravaganza in which Al sang a number of his own compositions.

WORMS

Jose Collins reached her zenith in *The Maid of the Mountains*, a musical comedy not written until 1917, when it played at the Winter Garden, London, she was already a star and an idol of Broadway audiences.

Although the songs that Al sang in *Vera Violetta*, numbers like 'That Haunting Melody' and 'Rum Tum Tiddle', have faded from public memory, his fellow performers long remembered Al's 'lively mind'. He never lacked ideas and often carried them out, to the invariable consternation of those who worked with him. During this show, he thought he might do better if he ran up and down the aisles as he sang, and proceeded to try the bizarre variation. To Al's delight, the audience loved it.

It was not long before his performing came to the notice of the Victor Talking Machine Co. They were astute enough to contract him to place his voice on wax for the very first time. His first recordings were made on 22 December 1911 and two of the titles chosen were 'That Haunting Melody' and 'Rum-Tum Tiddle' – thanks to Al's inimitable rendering, the most talked of, hummed to, songs in New York. 'That Haunting Melody' was written for him by another great artist, George M. Cohan and was an excellent vehicle for the great tenor quality of his voice – a point that the recording company made sure the public did not miss, by putting the words 'Tenor – Comedian' on the record label.

March 1912 saw the opening of *The Whirl Of Society* with Al and Stella Mayhew, his fellow blackface in *La Belle Paree*. One of the big numbers in the show was 'My Sumurun Girl' which Al and Stella sang as a duet. In *The Whirl Of Society*, for the first time, Al took the name on stage of 'Gus', one he was to use for many years. By this time, audiences knew Jolson and looked forward eagerly to his idiosyncratic act, with its compelling restlessness and limitless energy. All his life Al was restless, wanting to get on with the next project or put new life into an existing one. This accounts for the tremendous verve in his work. In the Jolson book, there was no such thing as 'taking it easy' – the only stage direction he understood was *allegro con brio*.

In 1913, he played in *Honeymoon Express* and in 1914, in *Dancing Around*. From 1911–1914, Al and company notched up four 'hit' shows, and he was the big gun, the success who shot those shows to the top. The Shuberts had done well when they took over his contract from Dockstader, and realised

Master of all he surveys, Al is seen here in *Bombo* (1921), presented by the Shuberts to open Al's own 59th Street Theatre.

now what it was that had glinted so richly under the blackface make-up of this golden boy.

During this time Harry Jolson continued as an established entertainer, and although he did not get the acclaim that his brother enjoyed, he was by no means taken lightly. The two brothers corresponded from time to time, but Al's nature was impetuous, and he would sometimes say things to his elder brother which would provoke a cool interlude. These differences, however, were always put right eventually.

The Shuberts and Harry understood well enough that Al was a big name, but their father could never quite appreciate that Al was a star, nor why Al should continue to put shoe polish on his face. The world of the cantor and that of his son were, indeed, vastly different; and Al's Jerusalem, in the cantor's eyes, had all the appearance of Babylon.

Al had further successes at the Winter Garden with *Robinson Crusoe* in 1916 and *Sinbad* in 1918, but it was in 1921 that the next great event in his life occurred. In that year, the Jolson Theatre opened on 59th Street. An entertainer must stand high in the public esteem before a theatre can carry his name as an almost permanent memorial to his art. Even more remarkable, it was only ten years since Al Jolson had first graced a Broadway stage as an unknown in musical comedy.

The show which opened with the theatre on 6 October was *Bombo*, a two-act extravaganza starring, of course, Al. The first night found him a bundle of nerves, paralysed with fear – he thought, larynx and all. A doctor was called to assure him that the famed 'Jolson Pipes' were in sound working order, but it took a great push by brother Harry – who had come to wish him well and had been standing in the wings – to get him on.

The reception from his audience was tremendous and Al, taking a deep breath, proceeded to give one of his greatest performances. That night he introduced the song 'April Showers', and left the audience holding a bombshell. After taking curtain call upon curtain call, he made a little speech saying in effect that the strain of first nights was getting too much, and that this would be his last show. The lives of his audience were not, however, destined to be shattered. There is no doubt that he meant what he said at the time but, next day, the notices of the critics made him change his mind.

Jolson was never content just to play to those who could afford a Broadway ticket, however, so he took his shows to the

The piercing, liquid eyes and eloquent, elegant hands in this fine portrait – one of Jolson's own favourites – sum up the man.

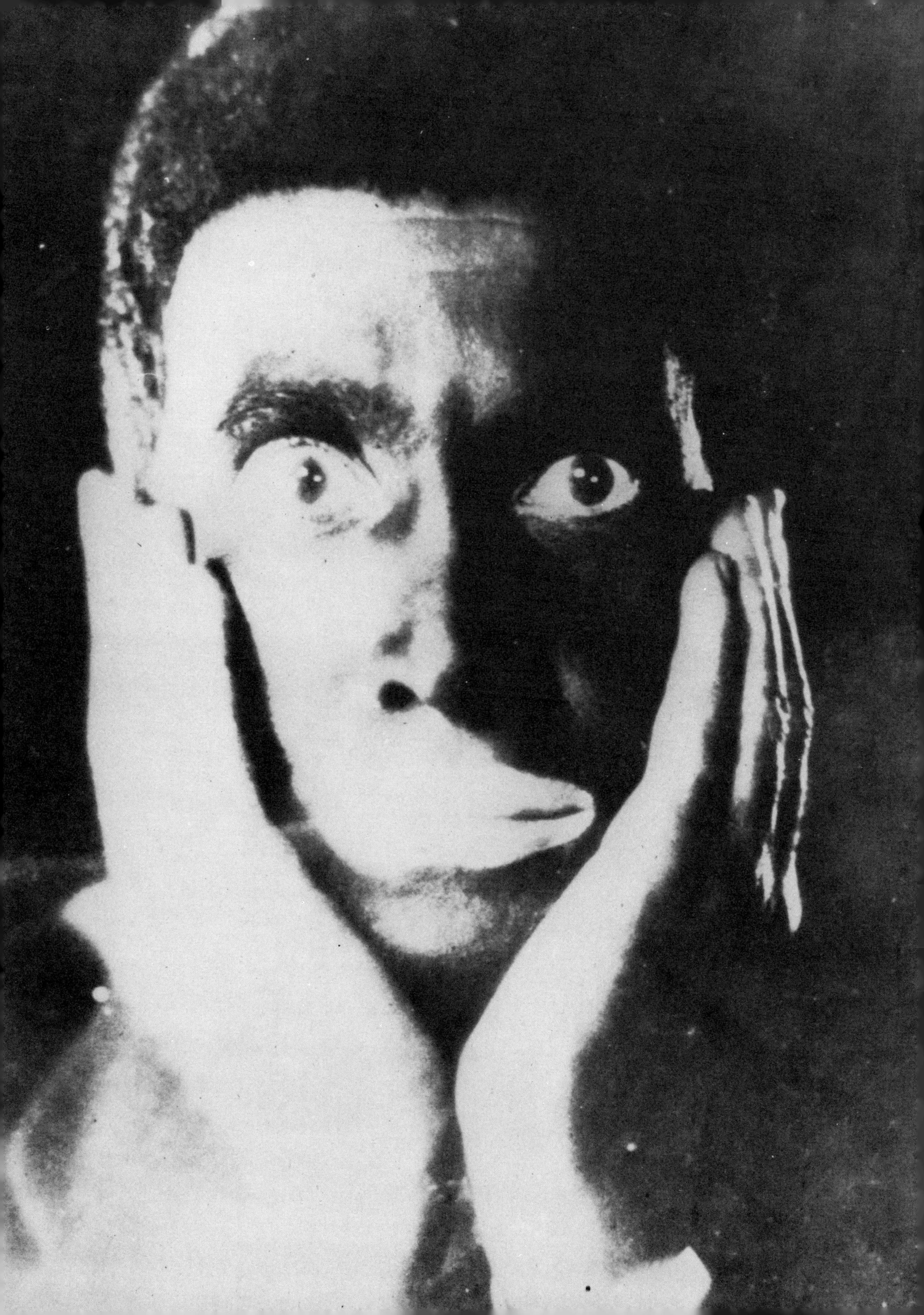

people. Suddenly, every town the length and breadth of America boasted its own Broadway. How else, he reasoned, were the people going to hear and see him singing songs like 'Swanee', 'Rockabye', 'My Mammy' and 'California Here I Come'. In a world that still revolved around thousands of tiny towns, that still lacked the communications which created the 'global village', he had good grounds for his claim that he was the world's greatest entertainer. He did after all test the truth of this apparently brazen statement before a huge number of people from vastly different backgrounds – and once they had heard him, nobody ever questioned it.

Although Al learnt his trade at a time when reaching your public, inside the theatre anyway, depended on the strength of your lungs, he nevertheless was happy to march in step with progress. Whenever he found himself in New York, he would go to the recording studios and sing into the large horns, with the very limited orchestra accompaniment that the system would allow. Some of his finest songs were placed onto wax from the stage shows of the period and few though they are in comparison with other artists' output, all his records are excellent, thanks to the magic of his projection. The spell-binding quality of his voice seemed to transcend the in-adequacies of primitive equipment and gave an immediacy to his singing that was only beggared by his live performances.

On 7 January 1925, Al Jolson presented another master-piece. This one was at the Winter Garden once again, as the theatre that bore his name was being used for Sigmund Romberg's *The Student Prince*. Al's show was called *Big Boy*, and he played the part of Gus, a Negro jockey who wins the Kentucky Derby. The show was packed with the usual collection of great songs his public came to expect from him – including 'California, Here I Come', reprised from a tour of his previous show, *Bombo*, in 1924. Among other songs like 'Hellow Tucky', 'Keep Smiling At Trouble', 'It All Depends On You', was one not today associated with Jolson, but he nevertheless introduced it. The song, 'If You Knew Susie', was given over to his great friend and rival Eddie Cantor, to have and to hold forever along with the fistful of Eddie's own hits. This song was taken up by others at the same time and so, apart from one sheet of music which records the fact of Al Jolson's big hit in *Big Boy* and which also bears his photo, the later prints of music read: 'The Hit of Five Productions – Al Jolson in *Big Boy*, Eddie Cantor in *Kid* [*Boots*], Willie

Howard in *Sky High*, Jack Rose in *Passing Show* and J. C. Flippen in *June Days*.' Apart from this instance of 'neglect', Al was still getting his well-earned praises. The *New York Times* had this to say after the first night:

In *Big Boy* Jolson seems to be even more vibrant and magnetic than ever before. He is all of the old Jolson, and something more of a new Jolson as well. A great man in the theatre is Mr Jolson, and everyone else was secondary, it was inevitable that he should be the most popular of them all.

Al was also still playing at the famous 'Sunday Night Winter Garden Shows' which he had instituted way back in 1913. The Shubert brothers would try all sorts of ploys to get Al back to these shows, no matter where he happened to be touring. A wire informing him that a rival had, in his absence, been a hit at one of the shows was usually enough to get him back to 'regain his throne'. All artists willingly performed at the Sunday concerts, whether it was entirely voluntary, as for a charity show, or because or they were a Shubert artist with this obligation written into their contract. It was the ultimate planetarium for the galaxy of stars that were in the ascendant then: Cantor, Jessell, the Marx Brothers, Fred and Adele Astaire, Ed Wynn and a host of others all played there, and the public flocked to them.

At this time, Al was sitting on top of his world. He was the idol of his profession, the idol of his public, the idol even of past and present Presidents. Though his stage life was a serene and fulfilled one, his private life was less happy. There are some like Eddie Cantor who meet with success profes-

Al was always generous with his time and money if he thought the cause was good; here he is seen (7th from left) at a benefit for destitute Russian artists held on 9 April 1922.

sionally, and also enjoy happy private lives, but Al was not so fortunate; the one real and lasting love in his life was the theatre.

Living and breathing the theatre, as he did, Al found the less heady air of home difficult to thrive on. Similarly, his wife found intolerable the atmosphere in which he was most happy. His marriage suffered and Henrietta, whom he had married in 1906, divorced him in 1919. She had always been the perfect wife and the perfect lady, and, as Al had climbed to fame, so she had done all in her power to be a credit to his name. But his love of the theatre, his love of his work to the

Unable to get into his own house on 59th Street, Al, playing Gus, opened in *Big Boy*, at the Winter Garden.

exclusion of all else, was bound to cause the breach. However, he and Henrietta remained friends long after the divorce. These were her wistful views on their relationship: 'When Al and I were poor we were always happy. Al was ambitious, and I was ambitious for him. I did everything possible for him to succeed. What did I gain? Nothing, I only lost him. The home was only a place for him to sleep. Yet I knew he would have loved a family of his own.'

Now Al was free to give his undivided self to the life of show business. He determined that there would be no more mistakes, no more frivolous digressions. He wasn't interested, he

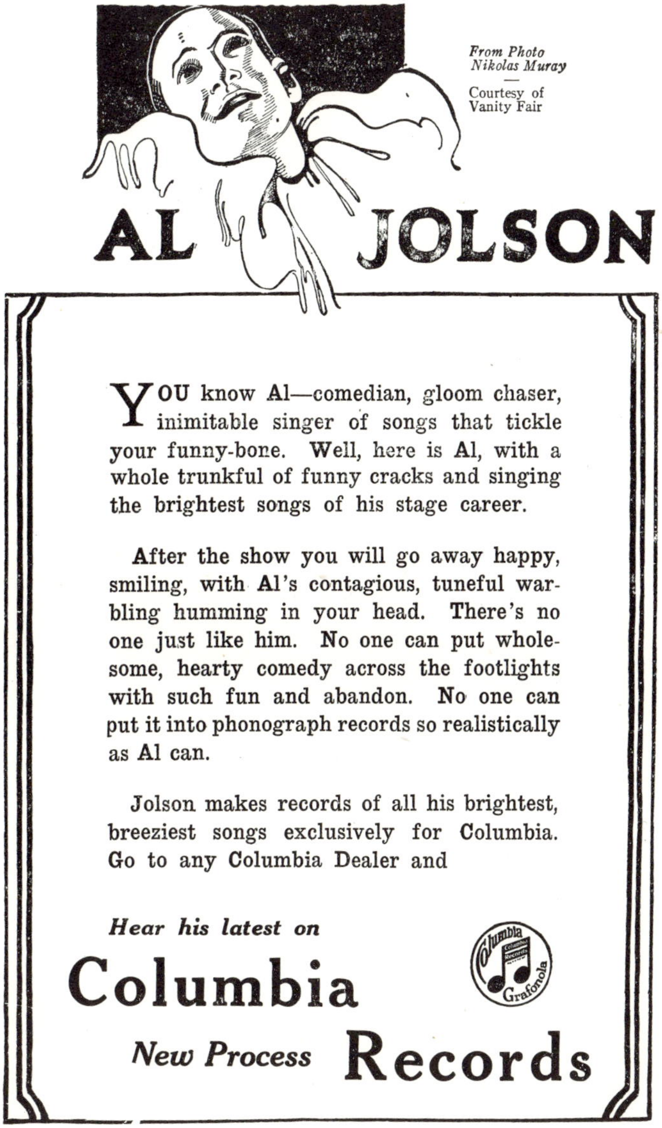

Al had early learnt the virtue of having many strings to his bow. This advertisement appeared on the back of a 1923 *Bombo* programme.

was wrapped up in his career. The restless Jolson was unfettered.

These resolutions did not, however, last long. Between 1919 and 1928, he was to be married twice more. His second marriage was to Alma Osborne, who was appearing in *George White's Scandals* under the stage name of Ethel Delmar. He came to her rescue at a party when someone was getting fresh, took her home and got married shortly afterwards. That was in the year 1922, and by 1926, Alma too had found that Al's love of the stage was too much of a rival. She divorced him.

Al foots it feetly with Patsy Kelly in *The Wonder Bar*, one show that did not open at the Winter Garden, but at the Nora Bayes Theatre.

Al was married again in 1928 – this time to Ruby Keeler whom he had first seen at Texas Guinan's night club. The partnership was consolidated when he later met her alighting from a train in Hollywood, at a reception for Fanny Brice. It seemed then that this was the perfect marriage. All his friends congratulated him on his choice. Unlike Henrietta, who was about the same age as Al, Ruby was only nineteen at the time, and perfectly sweet. She was a dancer by profession, and, despite her disparaging description of herself as a 'hoofer', a very talented one. Naturally Al saw to it that her talents were appreciated by the right sort of people.

When Florenz Ziegfeld presented his newest, most lavish spectacle – and nobody was ever more lavish than Ziegfeld – the star of the show, aptly called *Show Girl*, was Ruby Keeler. This pleased Al beyond words – he was the acclaim of Broadway and Ruby, the love of his life, was *the Show Girl*.

The night *Show Girl* opened in Boston in 1929 was a glittering occasion. Ruby, as Dixie Dugan, sang and danced her way through the show in the company of Jimmie Durante and Lou Clayton. Supplying the music for the three of them was none other than Duke Ellington. As Ruby came on and went into her dance routine to the George Gershwin song 'Liza', there was a great commotion in the audience. Her new husband came running down the aisle singing the chorus. This was an unexpected pleasure for the audience, and they loved it, as did the lady to whom this musical compliment was paid.

This impromptu act continued for the first week. In the wings, waiting to go on, Durante wryly asked, 'What's going to happen when Jolie ain't there to sing this song? It's marvellous when he sings it, but the nights he's not there, there'll be a difference.'

Al lullabies Davey Lee, picked by Al out of a horde of auditioning children, in a subdued little scene at the back of *The Singing Fool* set.

So welcome was this interruption to the show, that the

These placards tell their own story – the public is about to be treated to another spin-off from *The Jazz Singer* machine.

management of the theatre offered him a princely sum if he would continue the song in the aisles. He refused. *Show Girl* moved into New York in July. A few weeks later Ruby Keeler had to withdraw from the lead because of ill health, and her part was taken over by the talented Dorothy Stone. October of the same year saw the close of the show because of a general decline in box office takings. However, Gershwin's number 'Liza' was to remain a favourite with Jolson throughout the years.

The Jolsons continued their successful theatrical lives, and, thanks to her husband, Ruby achieved a fame that perhaps otherwise may not have been hers. From shows she went into films, making *Gold Diggers of 1933*, *Flirtation Walk* and then, in 1933, her best-known picture, *42nd Street*. With her in *42nd Street*, were Bebe Daniels, Dick Powell, Warner Baxter and George Brent, all of whom were to achieve fame in films.

In May 1935, Al and Ruby adopted a baby boy. In 1936, the Jolson-Keeler team reached the crest of its wave of fame, with a picture featuring both of them. In this film, called variously *Go Into Your Dance* or *Café De Paree*, they performed a song and dance number called 'About A Quarter To Nine'. This and the rest of her performance made Ruby Keeler a star in her own right. Al became jealous of her popularity, and, while hoping that her success would not wreck their

The maestro with the movie moguls – Al stands with Jack L. Warner and Darryl Zanuck beneath some imposing flying machinery of the late 1920s.

DUX
LIN

A distinguished reception committee for Fanny Brice (centre): Jack Warner, Darryl Zanuck, Archie Mayo and Al Jolson. It was at this reception in 1928 that Al met Ruby Keeler.

marriage, obviously found it difficult to live with. It was a great blow to Al when the marriage ended in the Paris Divorce Courts in December 1939. Everyone, including Al himself, now accepted that normal married life was not for this particular entertainer. The theatre public had finally claimed him for its own, and were never to let him go.

The emotional upheaval with Ruby Keeler brought on a bad bout of eczema which almost drove Al mad. In his frantic attempts to get away from people, he moved in and out of hotels so fast that it was almost impossible to keep up with him. But wherever he went, whatever he did to avoid people, the dreadful itch went with him. At last, in an obscure drug store, he found an ointment that did the trick. He had the ointment analysed, and this same mixture became known as 'Dr Jolson's Formula'.

Though the ointment was to cure many famous show-business names, perhaps one of the most startling instances of its success, and of Al's sympathetic nature, was the case of Walter Winchell. Between Jolson and this famous columnist, there had been a feud for years. On one occasion, Al was booked, at a huge salary, for a ten-week personal appearance tour with Harry Akst at the piano, opening at the Capitol Theatre, New York. He read an item a few days later in Winchell's column, observing that it was a shame that Al Jolson had to work on Yom Kippur (the sacred Jewish Day

From the big screen to the compass of a postage stamp, Al's face was everywhere, in this case commemorating a Motion Picture Anniversary issue.

of Atonement). Al was deeply hurt. He cancelled the whole tour and went off in search of Winchell. Finally catching up with him at Hollywood Legion Stadium, Al took a swing at him.

One day, not long after this bout of fisticuffs, 'Jolie', as he was often called, was lying in the sun at Palm Springs with the Hollywood reporter Irving Hoffman, who was also a friend of Winchell's. 'Say Al!' volunteered Hoffman, 'I hear Walt is in agony'. 'Thats good!' said Al. 'Going out of his mind too,' continued Hoffman. 'Great!' said Jolson tersely, 'that's just great!' 'An itch, he's got an unbearable itch,' said Hoffman. Al looked at Hoffman, then sat up, looking straight through him. 'Irv,' he said, 'I'm going to give you something to send to our mutual friend, but on one condition – that guy must never know where it came from.' With that he went off to his room for a jar of 'Dr Jolson's salve'. Hoffman duly sent the salve to Winchell and Winchell's itch was cured, but Hoffman couldn't resist telling Walter who the benefactor was. So overwhelmed with gratitude was Winchell, that the feud ended there and then.

This is a typical example of Al's instinctive generosity, and also of his passion for doing such favours anonymously. Few people knew who it was that financed the care of his manicurist's son, who was suffering from tuberculosis. Another beneficiary of his secret philanthropy was his cigarette salesman's child, who suffered from polio. These examples reveal a quiet thoughtfulness which few would connect with the livewire showman who stood under the spotlights.

The public examples of his generosity are legion: gifts to the Cedars of Lebanon Hospital; the financing of a tuberculosis ward in Monrovia; support for U.S.A. Boys' Homes – these and the wealth of private gifts reflect, perhaps, positive gratitude for his own good health and a sympathy, born of experience, for those who were not so lucky. Several articles indicate that Al had suffered from serious illness, including tuberculosis and pneumonia, early in his life. This is confirmed by the turn that events would take at the end.

Al Jolson became King of Broadway soon after he set foot on its hallowed boards, but he enjoyed no such smooth accession in the world of film. In 1923, he had started to make a silent film with D. W. Griffiths and had been horrified with what he saw. The film was never completed. For years, there had been experiments with talking pictures, but none of these had led anyone to believe the medium could ever be a commercial success. The silent film industry was at its peak, and had produced such stars as Douglas Fairbanks Senior, Mary Pickford, Vilma Banky, John Gilbert, and Rudolph Valentino. It was not a world that Al Jolson had mixed in much, though there is a curious story of how he helped Valentino, perhaps the silent-screen world's first citizen. During one of the Jolson Road Shows, Al was asked if there was a spare berth on the train. There was, and the ever-generous Al agreed at once to its being filled. The man who was privileged with this free ride was none other than Rudolph Valentino.

Apart from such passing encounters and one short venture, which we will come to a little later, Jolson had little to do with film until 1927 – just before another epoch-making event, Lindbergh's flight across the Atlantic. At that time, Warner Brothers were one of the major companies in Hollywood, yet financially they were in a bad way. They decided to stake everything on making the talking picture a success. The film was to be *The Jazz Singer*, a play that was running on Broadway with Georgie Jessel in the lead. Jessel himself was originally signed for the film version, but when he realised his voice was being actually recorded for sound purposes, he wanted more money, which Warners resented.

The company decided that Jessel was not for them and immediately phoned Eddie Cantor, who was playing the

Al adds City Hall to his Broadway kingdom when he is made Honorary Mayor of Encino, California in 1934.

A publicity still from *Hallelujah, I'm a Bum* (1933), which, as this shows, was tactfully changed to 'Tramp' for British audiences.

Al and his third wife Ruby Keeler pose serenely together at a function in 1935.

Orpheum in San Francisco. Cantor was reluctant to do *The Jazz Singer*. He felt sure that any trouble between Warners and Jessel could be smoothed out, and even volunteered to persuade Jessel to do the part when he saw him the following week. Unwilling to wait a moment longer to find their jazz singer, Warners phoned Jolson in Denver the next day. He at once agreed to take on the role.

Because of the tremendous gamble Warner Brothers were taking with the new venture, Jolson agreed to take no salary, arranging instead to take his money out of any profits that might be forthcoming. As things turned out profits did come, and it is estimated that his deal with Warners netted Al $700,000.

The Jazz Singer was the usual backstage story about the son of a Jewish cantor who upsets his father by performing in nightclubs, devoting all his time to singing instead of the synagogue. The plot of *The Jazz Singer* was of course, uncannily close to Jolson's own life story. In the film there was to

When you arrive, arrive in style – Al does just this at the Warner Brothers' lot in 1935.

be no dialogue, only the songs were to be recorded. These were the conditions laid down by Warners, but conditions were for other mortals, not Al Jolson. His continual, and irresistible, ad-libbing when the microphones were running made nonsense of the original plan. After his very first song, he quietened the clapping of the extras by telling them, 'You ain't heard nothin' yet,' and informing them that he would sing 'Toot, Toot, Tootsie Goo'bye' *and* whistle. As well as these enlivening modifications to the script, the film differed from the George Jessel stage play in that there the singer returned to the synagogue, whereas Al closed the film by singing 'My Mammy', so indicating his decision to stick to the stage.

When *The Jazz Singer* was shown in New York at ten dollars a head, the crowds rioted. Sound and the talkies were here to stay. Behind the triumph in New York, however, there was a cruelly ironic tragedy. On the night of the première there was an empty seat out front. Sam Warner had died that morning unaware that he had simultaneously made history and solved their financial problems.

The following morning in New York, the headlines of Variety declared:

CROWDS CHEER JOLSON PREMIERE
FIRST TALKING PICTURE SENSATION
REVOLUTION HITS SHOW BUSINESS
'JAZZ SINGER' MARKS END OF SILENT PICTURES

The Jazz Singer, however, had not been Al's first venture into sound films. Warners had, in 1926, already acquired the rights to use a system devised by Dr Lee Deforest, whereby sound was placed onto large discs. (These played at $33\frac{1}{3}$ revolutions per minute, like modern long-playing records but with much wider tracking.) The sound was then synchronized with the film on the screen. Warners called the process Vitaphone and built up a considerable library of one-reel shorts, using the talents of vaudeville, dance-band and even opera performers.

The tenor, Giovanni Martinelli, was the biggest offering to be shown at the very few cinemas that the Warner Brothers had equipped for this system, until, in 1926, they obtained the services of Al Jolson to make a short, which had its first showing at New York's Colony Theatre on 7 October 1926. It was initially called *A Plantation Act*, but later retitled *April*

Footprints in the sands of time, delicately placed by our hero – with some help – at Grauman's Chinese Restaurant (circa 1935).

Showers. In this one reeler were songs like 'April Showers', 'Rockabye Your Baby With A Dixie Melody' and 'When The Red Red Robin Comes Bob Bob Bobbin' Along'. The songs may have been good but the films themselves were primitive and the sound reproduction was, to say the least, not as we know it today. These films were meant to be treated just as a novelty by the public, and of course their silent rivals were still going strong at that time.

After *The Jazz Singer*, Al had an even bigger success with *The Singing Fool* – first shown at The Winter Garden on 19 September 1928, and introducing the deathless, unforgettable song 'Sonny Boy'. The original story had called for a little girl to play the child's part. Sixty had turned up for audition, all carefully primed and presented by their mothers. But Al, arriving a little late, felt a hand pulling at his coat, looked down, saw a cute little face looking up at him – and said, 'Hello, Sonny Boy! You're it.' That was the end of auditioning and it only remained to find a song, duly supplied by the song-writing team of DeSylva, Brown & Henderson. The recording, issued on the Brunswick label, sold by the million and dozens of other labels recorded their own artists singing the song. John McCormack and Gracie Fields both

Al and Ruby Keeler sun themselves in company with the baby boy they had adopted the year before in 1935.

recorded memorable versions but Al's version outstripped them all.

The film, of course, had other songs: 'It All Depends On You'; I'm Sitting On Top Of The World'; 'Golden Gate'; 'Keep Smiling At Trouble' – and one other song that landed Jolson and Warners with a law suit. It was 'The Spaniard That Blighted My Life'. This was written by British music hall artist Billy Merson in 1911 and had always been associated with him that side of the Atlantic. However, Al had introduced the song to America in 1913 as part of his stage show *The Honeymoon Express*. He was well away from Merson's stamping grounds, and copyright did not apply, besides which Al's songs were being sung in Britain well before his name was even 'known'. His song 'My Sumurun Girl', which he had co-authored in 1912, for example, was playing in British theatres that year. A little later, even bigger hits were brought over to Europe by American stars who had seen Jolson perform them. Miss Grace La Rue, in particular, scored a big hit in London when she sang 'You Made Me Love You' at the Palace Theatre in 1913. Miss Ethel Levey had a similar success in the show *Follow The Crowd* at the Empire Theatre in 1916. She sang 'Where Did Robinson

Having a flutter in style, Al discusses form in his own box at the Santa Anita Racetrack (1936).

Crusoe Go With Friday On Saturday Night' which was taken from Al's hit show of that year, *Robinson Crusoe*.

Billy Merson, however, realising that his song was to be on screen worldwide, felt that normal free-trading 'agreements' between artists did not apply in this case and he judged himself to have sole rights to the song. The courts, unfortunately for him, did not share his view. Not only did Merson lose the case but it cost him almost every penny he possessed, and ended his hopes of an early retirement. He was forced to tread the boards again, and worked right up to the time of his death.

While this court action was going on, the song was cut out of the film once and for all. This excision did not, however, prevent *The Singing Fool* from becoming the biggest box office earner of them all, until *Gone With The Wind* was issued in 1939. Nor, indeed, was the song entirely removed from Al's repertoire. On a tour of North Africa in 1943, he sang the 'Spaniard Song' to the troops, always prefacing it with a tribute to 'that Merson man of the Music Hall'. Later on in life, he was also to join Bing Crosby in a highly successful recording of this contentious number.

By taking the plunge into talkies when others had feared to tread, Jolson had added Hollywood to his Broadway kingdom, and, although there is no doubt about which of the two he considered to be 'home', he did himself, and a host of others, a lot of good by this annexation. As a result of the talkies' success, via Jolson, every studio rushed to bring other stars of vaudeville out to Hollywood, even the man who had passed up the chance of being 'first'. George Jessel made his first film, called *Lucky Boy*, in 1929. The response to that, however, was far less ecstatic that it had been to the two previous Jolson films, and it is debatable whether, if he had been the talkies' pioneer, the silent film would have disappeared so quickly from the public gaze.

The pleasures of sovereignty soon began to pall, however, and Hollywood was to prove a monstrous proposition for Al. The film plots were not the jolly affairs that they should have been, since Warner Brothers, keen to exploit Al's talent for pathos, always seemed to serve up lump-in-throat scripts. After *The Singing Fool* they brought back to life the child actor, who had 'died' in that picture, to play in the film, *Say It With Songs*. All the life that Al injected into the film by his vivacious rendition of the excellent songs was deadened by the mawkish script which the weepie plot demanded.

Martha Raye mimics the 'Mammy Singer' to the delight of the man himself. This animated, if contrived, tableau publicised their 1937 WABC/Columbia radio programme.

CBS

Two early films, both made in 1930, were, thankfully, exceptions to this rule of sentimentality. *Mammy*, built around a travelling minstrel troupe, and *Big Boy*, based on his stage success of 1925, were excellent vehicles for his talent. The latter film was particularly good because it gave Al the comedian as well as Al the singer, a chance to show his face, one that was covered in blackface make-up right up to the end of the film when, as the jockey 'Gus', he wins the race. Then he appeared whiteface on a stage with the full cast, and, after making a speech of thanks to his audience for watching the film, ended it with the song, 'Tomorrow Is Another Day'. In 1934, he made another picture based on the 1931 stage show *Wonder Bar*, which had been his first stage musical played without blacking up.

Jolson's biggest concern during this period was to further the career of his wife Ruby Keeler. However, there was little that he could do directly since her co-stars always seemed to be the Dick Powell types which the public were now demanding. Al contented himself with doing the odd concert which was offered him and also exploring another field of 'new' entertainment – radio. In this, he was rather a late-comer, getting his own series only in 1932, when he was sponsored by General Motors in *The Chevrolet Radio Show*.

It cannot be said that he immediately took to radio, for it seemed to him yet another invention designed to take him from the live audience he so loved. Instead of relying on instinct and experience, he was always having to keep one eye on the microphone and the other on the sponsor. Commercial radio did not care one way or another about the intricacies of show business. Their interest was in 'selling' the product, and Jolson, being, unlike many, extremely well heeled, could not be forced to lower his standards. From 1932 until 1943, he was to change sponsors five times, the best of them producing the *Shell Château* show of 1935–6 and the *Lifebuoy* shows of 1936–9. Even in the age of the crooner, Al still had his following, though it was diminished. He anyway seemed pretty thankful that the radio work gave him time to spend with his wife and adopted baby boy.

Although their professional paths diverged, Al did make a film with his wife in 1935. *Go Into Your Dance* was its name and it was very well received. He followed this, though not with her, with *The Singing Kid* in 1936, and, by 1939, had learned enough about being an actor to give a terrific perfor-

Two kings of show business, Al Jolson and Bing Crosby, enjoy the sport of kings together at Santa Anita Racetrack, 1938.

mance in *Rose Of Washington Square* – even if he did have to take billing below Alice Faye and Tyrone Power. Without the need of a single 'second take', he put over all his old favourite songs with splendid verve, and the film remains to this day a splendid example of vintage Jolson.

Swanee River was to be his last film appearance with the exception of *Rhapsody In Blue*. It told the story of Stephen Foster, one of America's finest popular song-writers of the last century. Jolson played the part of Christie, the founder of the Christie Minstrels in this all-colour film. In the final scene, after the death of Foster, Jolson sings the best loved of all Foster's songs, 'Swanee River'.

Al was to sing of this famous watercourse again on film,

Hold On To Your Hats was Al's last stage show, and one that, by its opening in 1940, had cost $100,000 of Al's own money.

Alice Faye and Tyrone Power, seen here with Al, took top billing in *Rose of Washington Square*, but Al's performance turned out to be second to none.

SAM S. SHUBERT THEATRE

CENTRAL THEATRES LEASING & CONSTRUCTION CO.

FIRE NOTICE: The exit, indicated by a red light and sign, nearest to the seat you occupy is the shortest route to the street.

In the event of fire or other emergency please do not run—WALK TO THAT EXIT.

JOHN J. McELLIGOTT, Fire Commissioner

THE · PLAYBILL · PUBLISHED · BY · THE · NEW · YORK · THEATRE · PROGRAM · CORPORATION

BEGINNING
MONDAY EVENING,
SEPTEMBER 16, 1940

It is urged for the comfort and safety of all, that theatre patrons refrain from lighting matches in this theatre.

MATINEES
WEDNESDAY AND
SATURDAY

AL JOLSON and GEORGE HALE

present

AL JOLSON

in

HOLD ON TO YOUR HATS

with

MARTHA RAYE   JACK WHITING   BERT GORDON

JOSEPH VITALE   GIL LAMB   RUSS BROWN   EUNICE HEALEY

Lyrics by E. Y. HARBURG

Music by BURTON LANE

Book by

GUY BOLTON   MATT BROOKS   EDDIE DAVIS

Book staged by Edgar MacGregor

Costumes and scenery by Raoul Pene Du Bois

Dances by Catherine Littlefield

Musical direction, Al Goodman

Entire production under personal supervision of GEORGE HALE

before leaving the medium for ever. In 1945, Hollywood made the film story of George Gershwin, a lifelong friend of Jolson. As a tribute to Gershwin, he appeared in *Rhapsody in Blue* as himself, and sang a Gershwin song which he himself had made famous, 'Swanee'. The part of Gershwin was played by Robert Alda, with Oscar Levant, also as himself, playing Gershwin's piano music – including 'Rhapsody In Blue' – and backed by Paul Whiteman with his band.

'Swanee' was not always a firm favourite with the public who eventually came to love it. It was one of the songs George Gershwin took to Ned Wayburn for the Capitol Theatre Show, and Wayburn took it without hesitation. How impressed he was may be guessed by the impressive setting he

In a sea of faces but bobbing up just the same, Al kids around after an impromptu show in the USA during August 1942.

Al suffering the little children with great good humour at the El Mitador Hotel, Palm Springs in 1939.

created for it as a production number, with sixty chorus girls and electric lights glowing from every shapely slipper. However, the audience reaction was at best lukewarm. The history of 'Swanee' might have ended at this point, but for the fact that the most magnetic star on the Broadway stage became interested in it. Jolson had just met Gershwin in Atlantic City, when *La, La, Lucile* was tried out there. They were introduced by Charles Previn, the conductor of the Gershwin Show. When Jolson gave an elaborate party at his penthouse in New York sometime later, he did not forget to invite the composer who had made such a good impression on him. Gershwin played through some of his songs, and when he came to 'Swanee', Jolson seized it at once, demanding it for one of his Winter Garden shows. Its first airing at one of the Sunday Night concerts, brought the house down. This tremendous reception encouraged him to interpolate it in the show *Sinbad*, where it stayed from 1918 until 1920. The audience's reaction this time was nothing less than tumultuous. The song caught on, winging across the whole country. So when the film *Rhapsody In Blue* was made, what better tribute could Jolson make than the singing of this old song. Later the same song was used again, and was still sufficiently popular to receive flattering treatment in *The Jolson Story* and, even later, to be used by Judy Garland as a production number in the film *A Star Is Born*.

Jolson always took a great interest in the work Gershwin wrote and produced. One day in 1933, Dubose Hayward called on Gershwin, saying that Jerome Kern and Oscar Hammerstein II wished to adapt his *Porgy* into a musical for Al Jolson. It seems that Jolson had long expressed an interest in the play for himself, and had even used part of it for one of his broadcasts. As things turned out, Jolson was never to be associated with the work which eventually became *Porgy and Bess*.

On Sunday 11 July 1937 at 10.35 a.m. George Gershwin died. The service was held at Temple Emanu-El on Fifth Avenue, New York. Despite a heavy downpour, almost four thousand of Gershwin's friends and admirers crowded into the Temple, while another thousand lined both sides of Fifth Avenue. Many of those who had tickets for the service were unable to get through the crowds. Jolson was one of these. It was not until a few friends had forged a path for him that he was able to get inside. Jolson, Mayor La Guardia, Walter

Al pauses with his hand baggage to pose with Merle Oberon, Patricia Morison and the pilot of the plane. The date: September 1942. The trio were off on a flying visit to entertain GIs in Britain.

Demerash, George M. Cohan, Edwin Franke, Goldman, Gene Buck, Vernon Duke, James J. Walker and Sam Harris (both of them former Mayors) acted as pallbearers, carrying the flower-covered coffin out of the Temple, to the strains of the slow section of 'Rhapsody In Blue'.

On 8 September 1937, a George Gershwin Memorial Concert, was held at the Hollywood Bowl, with a great number of musicians and stars taking part. The conductors were Otto Klemperer, and Nathaniel Shilkret with Victor Young. Al Jolson again sang 'Swanee' as a tribute to his old friend, and Oscar Levant, too, was on the programme.

When *Wonder Bar* closed in 1931, Al Jolson suffered his first decline in popularity. Since his instant success with *La Belle Paree* at the Shubert Theatre in 1911, he had been the unchallenged idol of Broadway, his title of 'The King' unchallenged. For over twenty years, the 'Great White Way' had been his. Suddenly it all changed.

Only two years previously, in 1929, at a dinner given in his honour, it had been stated by the Master of Ceremonies that it seemed as though the name of Al Jolson had always been in lights on Broadway, and that none could envisage a time when Broadway would be without its 'King'. It is difficult to give the reason for this change of events. Largely it was brought about by himself. When he closed *Big Boy*, he went off to Hollywood to make *The Jazz Singer*. Over the next eleven years, he only twice appeared on the Broadway stage with *Wonder Bar* and *Hold On To Your Hats*.

He was away too long. Granted he had been in the public eye with his films, and there is no doubt that the first two were among the wonders of the century. As an entertainer he stood supreme, but was this so as an actor in pictures? The answer is no. By 1930, talking pictures were accepted, and a new crop of actors, and fine actors at that, had moved in on this new medium. Every year saw vast improvements in the film industry, and, even in the early thirties, *The Jazz Singer* and *The Singing Fool* were spoken of as the 'first talkies', remarkable only for that fact. Nevertheless the Jolson films continued to be crowd-drawers, every one of them, and still he was being pushed out.

Along with the decline in demand for Al's performance, his records also showed a drop in sales. 'Sonny Boy' and 'Mammy' sold well over the million mark each and his recording experience went back as far as 1911. From that

Revueing the men – Al entertains a contingent of the 2nd US Armored Division in Sicily during November 1943.

time on, for a good number of years, he was always way ahead of the others, selling unprecedented numbers of records.

In this case, Al's waning popularity cannot be explained by his own actions. He may have invited deposition from his Broadway kingdom by his neglect of the public, but his behaviour obviously did not have such a strong bearing on the sale of records already made. The simple fact is that public leisure habits and public taste had changed. When Al cut his first records, listening to music was only a part of enjoying music at home; people still played it. It was a regular practice to sell sheet music in theatre foyers, so that the audience could go home and play and sing what it had just heard on the stage. Since Al wrote many of the songs that he presented on stage, the sale of sheet music was a part of his income, as well as an assurance to him that his kind of public

A.V.C.
A Salute
It Is An Honor for A.V.C.
in behalf of the men and women in the armed forces who won our fight for freedom,
to salute their outstanding friend
Mr. Al. Jolson
During the days of pain, loneliness and boredom this great entertainer cheered millions of us who were scattered over the earth. Every theatre of war was brightened by his presence.
Charles G. Bolte, chairman
American Veterans Committee
In the presence of more than 1,000 fellow-citizens at the hotel Astor, New York City, October 1, 1946.

Smoking can damage your health, but the smiling caricature on a British cigarette card confirms that singing is good for you.

One Yank's thanks speak for many. In October 1946 Sergeant Oretsky presents a scroll to Al on behalf of the American Veterans Committee at a testimonial dinner in New York.

still existed. With the advent of radio and television, however, domestic music production was no longer necessary. A song could be heard in millions of homes simultaneously, without the necessity of a piano or even a gramophone being played in a single house.

The other important reason for the decline in his popularity was that a different style of singing had come into vogue. Although it had been a slow process, starting as early as 1925, the crooner had finally staked a firm claim on the public's affections. And just as Al had been a trail-blazer in his day, so the crooners had a man by the name of Bing Crosby to pave the way for them.

Al could not, of course, change his style of singing, but he did make some attempt to come to terms with the world's new toy. As we have seen, he flirted, rather fractiously, with radio during the thirties, but was not a great success. He needed a live audience to recharge his own batteries, and, for the audience's part, the disembodied voice was a poor substitute for his pulsating stage presence.

Despite these changes, it would be folly to imagine that his decline meant the end of the Al Jolson that really was the World's Greatest Entertainer – Al Jolson, the stage performer. There were many occasions when he would be called upon to appear, and meet with standing ovations, just as he did through his great years. Proof of that was given in 1935 when he attended a benefit concert in New York. The audience was 12,000 strong. Al Jolson sang his first song, 'Sonny Boy', to the accompaniment of Benny Goodman, and took six curtain-calls for his trouble. This was just for the first song, and was proof positive that he was still appreciated in certain quarters. Another indication of his standing – and his need to be loved – is the story of C. B. Cochrane, the doyen of British impressarios, who had seen Al work many times, and enjoyed his style. In general Cochrane had no time at all for the sentimental singing manner but he thought Jolson had the most wonderful style in the world. So profound was his admiration, that, in the thirties, he invited him to appear as a one-man show at the Royal Albert Hall in London. Jolson however refused, explaining, 'In New York I am an idol, if I came to London, I may flop. I could never face an audience again. Here I am King.'

Jolson would, of course, have been as big a sensation in England as he had been in America. His admirers came from all walks of life, from Al Capone to the President of the United States. He was President Harding's favourite entertainer, and was a frequent guest at the White House. London would have loved him.

Al may have felt vulnerable about his audience appeal but, financially, he had no worries. Although he had never been a saver at any time, his earnings from the stage, screen and recordings were simply enormous. The fact was that money came in so quickly he was unable to spend it. He had also made some excellent investments, and when the Wall Street crash came in 1929, he came out of it unscathed. These investments had, admittedly, been made in the twenties much against his own judgement, but on the sound advice of friends. However he managed to hang on to what earned, it worked, and his wealth was often a cause for joking amongst those who knew him sufficiently well.

Money, as is so often observed, is not everything, and Al, it must be said, had fallen on evil days. It was painful for him to recall his heyday at the Winter Garden when he would sometimes bring the show to a close, and then carry on with a one-man show instead. He would nostalgically recall the time that he was asked about the extra cost of paying the electricians and stage hands overtime. His reply: 'Overtime, sure they get paid overtime, but that's not all they get. They get me, and I see 'em standing in the wings enjoying every minute I'm out there.' Ironically, the tables had been turned. It was Al who stood in the wings, while the centre of the show business stage was held by the technicians who now controlled the people's pleasure.

During this period, Al saw his brother Harry more often than he had previously, and Harry knew how much this peripheral role was eating into him. 'Cheer up brother,' Harry would say, 'you've been up there before, and stayed for a long time. You'll be up there again, greater than ever. You'll see.' As at the time when his voice had broken, Al wasn't convinced. But, Harry's comforting words had been right then and his words rang true now, and were to echo far beyond Al's wildest dreams.

Hold Onto Your Hats in 1940, was the world's last chance to see Jolson in a stage show. Such was the lack of interest in backing this old 'pro', that he had to whistle up his own backing – to the tune of $100,000 – and take on a co-producer by the name of George Hale.

Georgie Jessel and Al chat during a radio rehearsal. Jessel was the man who turned down the chance of filming *The Jazz Singer* when he was already starring in the stage show.

Al under the surveillance of a youngish-looking John Edgar Hoover, head of the FBI, at the Stork Club. He appears to be explaining himself to Mr Hoover's satisfaction.

Jimmy Durante peevishly accuses Al of twisting his words in this knockabout sequence captured during a radio rehearsal.

The show, based around a singing cowboy radio star, had a six-week pre-Broadway run in Chicago. Al had hired his, by now, ex-wife Ruby Keeler to take the female lead, but she apparently found it 'difficult' to work alongside Al and left. Her part was taken by Eunice Healey and the show reached the Shubert Theatre and Broadway on 11 September 1940. Other performers of note in the show were Martha Raye, Bert Gordon (The Mad Russian), and Jinx Falkenberg. Here was the old Jolson back, at last, in his element. If the story wasn't of the best, he made good use of the songs and comedy. For good measure, after every performance he sang requests of his old hit numbers, often keeping his audience on for as much as two hours. Al loved it, of course. It was the breath of life for him, and, for his audience, an invigorating spectacle of real showmanship.

Unfortunately, he worked himself beyond even his great staying powers, and illness eventually forced him to close the show on the first day of February 1941. He then went off to Florida to regain his health. Fittingly, although the show was a success, there was no one to be an understudy for Al Jolson.

At this point in his life, Al Jolson could well have faded from the scene for ever, and his name been relegated to the history books. However, that dame Providence, who had looked so kindly on him in the past, was preparing a stage for him just over the horizon that would bring in an audience to dwarf all his earlier houses. Al was about to enter an entirely different kind of theatre – the theatre of the most destructive war the world had ever known.

When America went to war, Al was fifty-six years old. The war clouds had been throwing down their deluge of death in Europe since 1939, and Al realised that his own country and everyone else's was to go through a terrible time. It seemed

Old enough to be their father, but still very much one of the boys, Al swops gags with Bob Hope (also sitting) at Hope's testimonial dinner given by the Friar's Club. Also cracking wise are Jessel, Benny, Cantor, Burns and Kyser.

the inevitable conclusion of a hell-bent decade. If the thirties had not been good years for Al, how much harder had they struck everyone else. America had been harried by gangsterism, England crippled by strikes, Germany corrupted by the rise of a single madman – and the whole world caught in the grip of economic depression.

Although America was not directly involved until the bombing of Pearl Harbour in 1941, all Americans, Al included, came to realise that it would eventually become America's war as well. It seemed, above all, a time for the young and healthy.

All his life Al had worried about his health. From his earliest childhood, he had been in constant fear of tuber-

Al tunes up for a song at the Friars Club testimonial dinner for Ronald Reagan as comedians Lou Holtz (left) and Ed Wynn look on.

culosis, and the slightest cough alarmed him. So strong was this feeling, that he diverted some of his royaltics to the Tubercular Hospital at Saranac Lake, New York.

Al never seemed happier than when riding in an open car under the desert sun of the California he loved so much. There he would be stripped to the waist. He had a passion for sunshine, and an intense preoccupation with keeping fit. During his later years he had become a little hard of hearing and would miss the odd word here and there, but would always let the remark go by, rather than have it repeated for his benefit. Friends marvelled at Al's sound teeth; if a bottle opener was not handy, off would come the top with his teeth. But few knew that towards the end he was using hair blackener each morning, with the same regularity that he used his toothbrush.

Al Jolson was a man obsessed with health out of his fear of losing it. He was also a man who loved audiences – of any kind – a man who bathed in their love. Their attention was positively therapeutic: he might be walking in a leisurely fashion up Fifth Avenue when he would hear a voice saying, 'Isn't that Al Jolson?' Up would go his shoulders, off came the glasses, the pace quickened, and Jolie would be bounding away like the young colt he no longer was. He was always on stage, always out front for his audience. Just as he swaggered through his songs, so he would give the appearance of swaggering through life. Al Jolson was the eternal showman. So the man who needed audiences but seemed to have been deserted by them, and who loved his country but could not fight for it, did what seemed most obvious to him. At fifty-six, he was too old to be a private soldier, but young enough to be the world's greatest entertainer. He would go and see how the boys of the U.S. Army liked his act.

He began by playing the camps at home, and the troops liked him. Jolson loved it and felt all the old suppleness returning to limbs and larynx. He was feeling better and fitter than he had been for years – he was back at work. He reasoned that if he could sing at home, he could sing overseas, and so he made history by being the first American entertainer to go overseas in World War II. Soon afterwards, he was followed by many other big names, including Crosby, Fred Astaire and Bob Hope. But it was Jolson once more who blazed the trail, who called the tune.

A man of many parts – most of them harmonious – Al tickles the ivories animatedly for the NBC publicity machine.

Milena Miller only appeared briefly as supporting singer with Al in Kraft Music Hall, but she, like many before her, seems to enjoy the privilege.

To many of the troops, he was unknown, indeed he had been known better to their grandmothers. However, he came from home, and that mattered greatly to the troops. On one occasion, he had just been introduced by the compère of the camp show, but elaborated in his own inimitable way: 'In case you don't know, I sing, maybe a kind of singing that you have never heard before, but, for old times' sake, I'd like to give you a song or two in the way we used to do 'em.' The 'way we used to do 'em' proved quite as good as anything that had succeeded it. His young audiences were presented, most of them for the first time, with an instinctive showman, who fed off their enjoyment to maintain energy and who intuitively gauged his act by smelling their mood.

For Al, it was just like the old days, as song followed song in an inexhaustible stream. His stamina on a good night was

Mirror, mirror on the wall, who has the biggest mouth of them all? Edgar Bergen and his toffee-nosed colleague, Charlie McCordy, gape happily with Al.

truly superhuman, as the story of George Jessel and Al at a big benefit concert admirably illustrates. Jessel, as M.C., introduced Al, who with his almost customary 'Alright folks, you ain't heard nothin' yet', proceeded to sing song after song.

Finally, Jessel, unable to stand it any longer, dropped his trousers to the floor and, walking onto the stage, exclaimed to the audience, 'Folks, you ain't seen nothin' yet.'

The soldiers did not need any such impromptu stripteases, Al was a stunning success with them right from the start. He covered many thousands of miles doing his one-man shows, performing the familiar songs night after night in the open, with only a piano for accompaniment. Once more, 'The King' was with his troops, each live audience inspiring life in him. The emotional chemistry of artist and audience was not enough, however, to counteract the killing pace. The tremendous number of shows performed, the number of miles covered, in all kinds of weather, began to tell on the not so young Jolson. Unknown to him at this time, the malaria germs picked up at Bathurst in West Africa had already begun to incubate in him, and he became feverish.

There was only one course left open to him, to return home. For the present, the old warrior was down, though by no means out. When he returned to the United States in 1943, after a gruelling tour of the war zones of three continents, Al was really debilitated. The tour had taken more out of him than he knew. On his 'tour of duty', he had worked as hard as any of the GIs that he had striven so hard to entertain.

Al, however, did not count the cost. For the past two years, since he had been back with his 'first love', he had begun to live again. It may not have been Broadway, but, to him, winning the hearts of the toughest, most worthwhile audience in the world was a greater pleasure. Because Al had none of the comforts, or distractions, of marriage, home or family and was, at this juncture, a lonely man, he returned to work soon after his return home. This time he was entertaining wounded veterans at a hospital in Sulphur Springs. The head doctor had said to Al, 'Eastman Annexe in Hot Springs is a little off the beaten track, but the boys there haven't had a live show in a long time. It would be wonderful if you could find time to make the run down there.'

'Find time', said Al briefly, 'we'll make time.'

It was after the show at Eastman Annexe, when Al was signing autographs for a long line of fans, that a lovely face

Al's Music Hall show drew many big names, among them Judy Garland, seen here rehearsing with him.

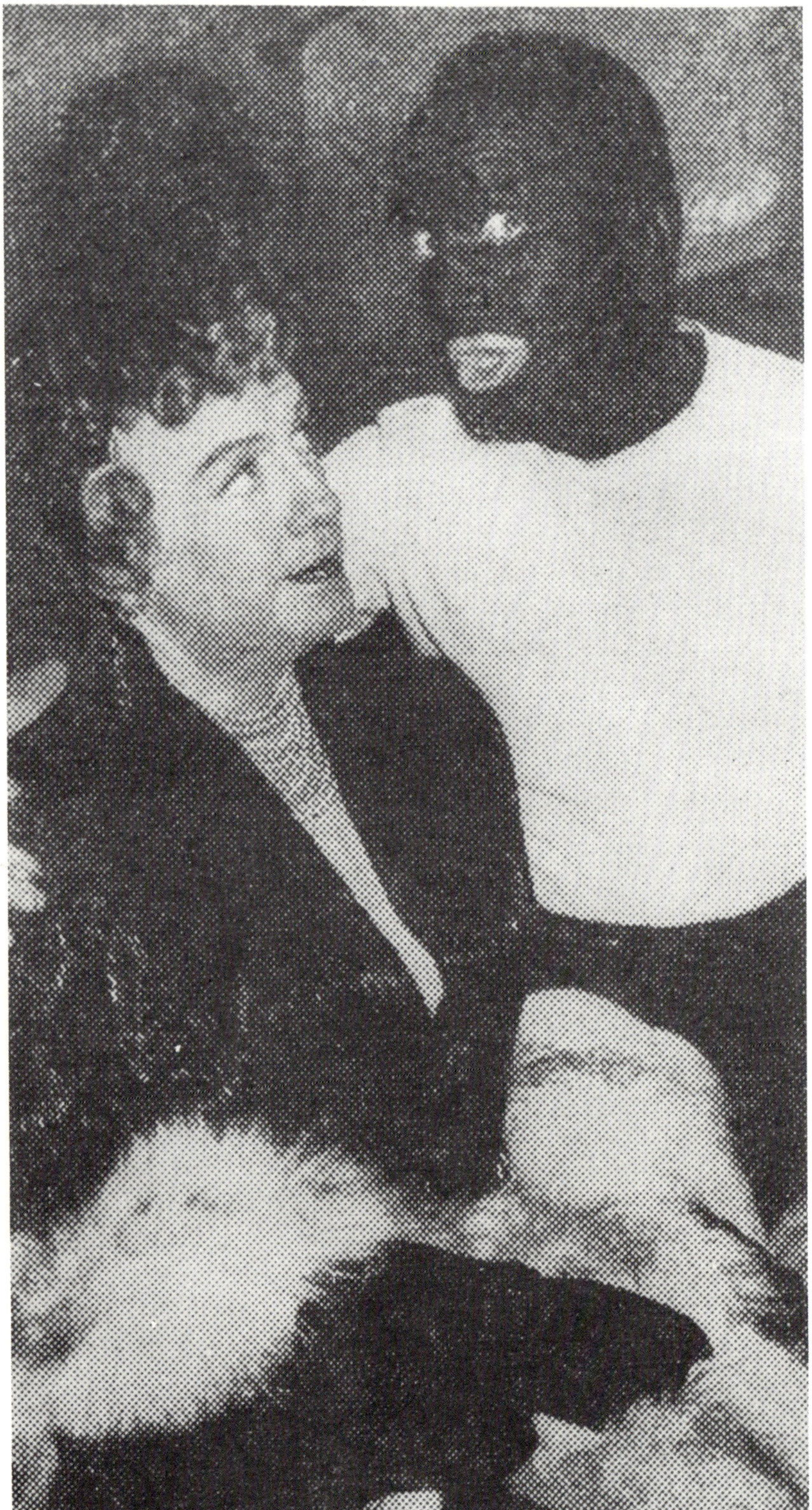

That ain't no lady, that is in fact Jack Benny being wooed by Al at a Friars Club frolic.

and shapely hand suddenly arrested his gaze. Now Al had a vocabulary all his own, in which anything that was bad was 'mogo on the gogo', anyone striking, 'a mouse's ear', and someone extra special, 'a marmoset's niece'. The owner of the lovely face and fair hand was very definitely 'a marmoset's niece' and one that obstinately refused to be dislodged from his mind.

On 23 March 1945, eight months after meeting Erle Galbraith, a civilian X-Ray technician attached to the army and navy hospital, he married her in the little town of Quartzite, Arizona. It was only a little over two months since he had collapsed once again, and this time had two ribs and most of his left lung removed. He was so near death's door that Associated Press released biographical details, for the 'impending obituary'.

However, Al's will power and Erle's love pulled him through and cheated the newshounds. He was still a sick man when he made his contribution to *Rhapsody In Blue*, but fully recovered in time to take his young bride to the June première in Hollywood. For Al, his marriage and the great revival of public interest in his talent were to make the next five years the happiest of his whole life.

Bing Crosby and Al had struck sparks off each other in their respective radio shows. Here Bing is a guest on Al's Music Hall show.

For his historians, these years were perhaps the most remarkable of his whole extraordinary life. He was, after all, a man in his sixties, who had just got married, had returned to work and whose legend was about to be recorded on celluloid. It was at this time that Harry Cohn of Columbia was persuaded by the columnist Sidney Skolsky to make the film biography of Jolson. *The Jolson Story* was a howling success, and led to a resurgence of Al's popularity beyond even the fevered imagination of a publicity agent.

This development did not, however, mean that Al simply collected the profits and basked in the glory. Not only had he been on the set nearly every day, advising as well as recording songs for the film, but he found that, as he knew so well anyway, *noblesse oblige*. He went on promotional tours and Savings Bonds drives, filled the principal guest spot on other stars' shows, made his own series of seventy-two shows, each half an hour long, for N.B.C. – and drew the kind of crowds that only the Jolsons, Crosbys, Presleys and Sinatras of this world can draw. He already knew that he was great but it must have been gratifying to have it confirmed. While Jolson slipped easily back into life at the top, Larry Parks was making the sequel to *The Jolson Story*.

This film sequel, called *Jolson Sings Again*, ensured that Jolsonmania continued at home and the tide of politics made sure that his name was kept alive abroad; for Jolson was on the move again. U.S. soldiers were at war in Korea, and Al, having been the first American entertainer to play to the troops overseas in World War II, wanted to be first again. However, he got no reply to the wire he sent President Truman in June 1950. Five weeks had gone by when he received a telegram from Secretary of Defense Louis Johnson, informing him that U.S.O., the war-time organisation for entertainment, was no longer active, and therefore no funds existed for this venture. Nothing daunted, Al decided he would entertain those boys if he had to pay his own passage. This is exactly what he did.

Jolson wanted his lifelong friend and piano accompanist, Harry Akst, to go with him on this trip, but Harry at first refused. He had been with Al in 1943, on his tours of South America, Africa and the Near East, and he had seen then the price Al had had to pay for those tours. Harry thought Al was too old now to stand the strain. He hoped, if he refused to go this time, that Al would not go without him.

Oscar Levant (left), musical director Lou Bring and Al chew the fat while working on Kraft Music Hall.

Jolson was adamant and declared that he would get someone else in Harry's stead, but, after a call from the head of the Morris Agency, Akst eventually relented. Jolson never could ask a favour of anyone and Akst realised that, however much Al wanted his friend along, he would never try to persuade him if he didn't want to go.

Harry called Al's wife, Erle, to let her know that he would be going with Al. She too was against the whole venture but neither of them could persuade Al not to go. He was incorrigibly restless and, this time, his natural restlessness was increased by his overwhelming urge to do something for the GIs. He was determined to show everyone, including himself, that Jolson was sixty-four years young.

In this atmosphere of fanatical determination from Al and great anxiety from everyone else, the final trip began – the trip that was to be the crowning glory in Jolie's triumphant comeback. There is no doubt, however, that the next three weeks were also to be the most gruelling he had ever been through. Jolson, now in his middle sixties, the age of retirement, was taking on a task that would have taxed the strength of a man half his age.

On a balmy evening in September, Al left for Los Angeles airport accompanied by his wife and Asa, the little son that he and Erle had adopted in January 1948. On the way, they collected Harry Akst. Al was dressed in his usual dashing version of army uniform, with an old white ski cap, a hunting jacket, and a pair of high boots out of the second act of *Hold Onto Your Hats* to round the whole outfit off. Erle was worried and asked Harry to take good care of Al. He reassured her and said it would more likely be a case of Al taking care of him.

Al and Harry travelled overnight to Honolulu, then flew on the next day over the Pacific. With them on the plane was Carl 'Tookey' Spatz, a retired Air Force General, whom they had last seen at General Dwight D. Eisenhower's headquarters in Algiers back in 1943. General Spatz was headed for the Far East as a war correspondent. Seeing Spatz again

Al and his new bride Erle Galbraith Jolson arrive from California to attend the New York premiére of *Rhapsody In Blue* in 1945.

Musical director Lou Bring (left) and producer Ezra McIntosh show Al the way – something he was unused to, but had to suffer in radio – in rehearsal for a July 1948 radio show.

Gary Cooper
Dottie Lamour
Halop
Eddie Green

reminded Harry that, when Al left New York in that summer of '43 for his trail-blazing tour of the war zone, he carried with him a letter from Mrs Eisenhower to her husband, which he was determined to deliver to 'Ike' in person. After doing shows in Dakar, Marrakesh, Casablanca and Oran, they had finally caught up with the High Command in Algiers. Eisenhower was, at the time, involved with the North African campaign, and a jungle of red tape had to be penetrated before Al and Harry were finally ushered into his presence. Al gave Eisenhower the letter from his wife, and watched while he opened and read it. The General told them that the letter contained a message to Al from Mrs Eisenhower. She asked him to give her husband a kiss for her, and also a kick in the pants for not writing more often. Eisenhower told Al he could 'cash in' the kiss when he saw Mrs Eisenhower in Washington, but as to the rest . . . . The General left his sentence unfinished, turned and lifted his coat tail. Sure enough, Al delivered the rest of the message by foot!

Now on their way to another continent, in another year and another war, Harry thought back to the start of that other trip. They had been rehearsing before their first show in World War II, in Georgetown, Guyana, when Harry noticed that Al was having trouble with the high notes at the end of 'Swanee'. Harry forebore to comment but Al was alarmed. He asked if the problem note was an 'F' and, when Harry said that it was, wanted to know why he couldn't hit it any more. Harry told him to relax, that the high notes weren't necessary with the advent of microphones and loudspeakers. The ending could easily be taken down a couple of tones. This indulgent compromise was no comfort to Al, however, and would have been an intolerable admission that Jolson was losing the high notes. Without being up with the mountain peaks, how could he sing 'Sonny Boy' or 'Mammy'? Al was ready to give up the whole tour. Harry used every argument to sell Jolson to Jolson all over again. Bing Crosby didn't rely on high notes and a high finish, he pointed out. The king of the crooners relied instead on the beauty of the resonance in his low tones. Al had resonance to spare and could do it too. High finishes anyway went out with vaudeville.

Eventually Al agreed to try a chorus of 'April Showers' in the key of 'D', and the result was superb. There and then in Georgetown, a new Al Jolson had been born. He went on to thrill the GIs of battle camps in three continents and when,

Ed 'Archie' Gardner towers genially over Al during a NBC Kraft Music Hall show on 5 February 1948.

subsequently, he made the sound tracks for *The Jolson Story* and *Jolson Sings Again*, it was the new Jolson who sang, in all his resonant beauty.

The plane bearing Al and Harry to Tokyo, en route for Korea, came down at Wake Island with engine trouble. They were forced to spend the night there in a damp, draughty hut, lying in the top bunks because the place was infested with rats from the days of the Japanese occupation. The old war dog Spatz slept like a baby, but Al and Harry wrestled with sleeping pills, and, when morning came, both had miserable colds and hacking coughs.

On 8 September 1950, Al and Harry coughed their way

Al puts Larry Parkes through his paces on the set. Al barely missed a single hour of the shooting of *The Jolson Story*.

into Tokyo and went straight to the Imperial Hotel where Al did not even wait to unpack but asked, in a hoarse voice, for the nearest hospital. They were guided to the army dispensary three blocks away, and there a young army doctor, peering down the famous throat, whispered to a colleague that he did not think this man would be able to sing. Al, who had overheard the conversation, stated that he *had* to sing. The doctors resignedly put him in a cabinet, draped a turkish towel over his head, and let him sit there for thirty minutes breathing mentholated steam. During the next few days, Al virtually lived in that cabinet.

The first show was in the courtyard of a Tokyo army hospital and Jolie wasn't sure if he was going to be able to go through with it. He stood by the piano looking out at the sea of men thronging the balconies and lawns, both Korean casualties and boys from back home. His severe, bronchial infection seemed a nitpicking complaint compared to the injuries some of these men had.

Harry sensed what he was thinking and suggested he told them a few stories first to save his voice. This Jolie did, first one, then another and another. Now they were laughing and Al was taking heart. He decided that if he could talk, he could sing, so he sang 'Swanee' and, encouraged by this, 'April Showers' – now he was warming up, so he sang 'Mammy', then 'Sonny Boy' and there was no stopping him now. For forty minutes he sang to them, they loved him and he thrived on their adulation. When it was over, however, Al returned to the dispensary and the choking mentholated steam. The next show was at 361st Hospital, where Jolie came to the same triumphant finale – by the same tentative stages. In all he did forty-two performances, completing his entire Far East itinerary by the same recipe: a song, a cough, a gasp of steam, and another song.

A note of pathos entered the tour at Iwokuni where the show was held in the mess hall. The Australian contingent had lost their Wing Commander that day and they were heartbroken. Al had to go outside, coax them into the mess hall, then work on them till, at last, he had them smiling through their tears.

The day before they left Japan, Al and Harry lunched with General MacArthur and his wife. When they arrived at the old American Embassy, Mrs MacArthur led them into the huge living room and made them feel completely at home.

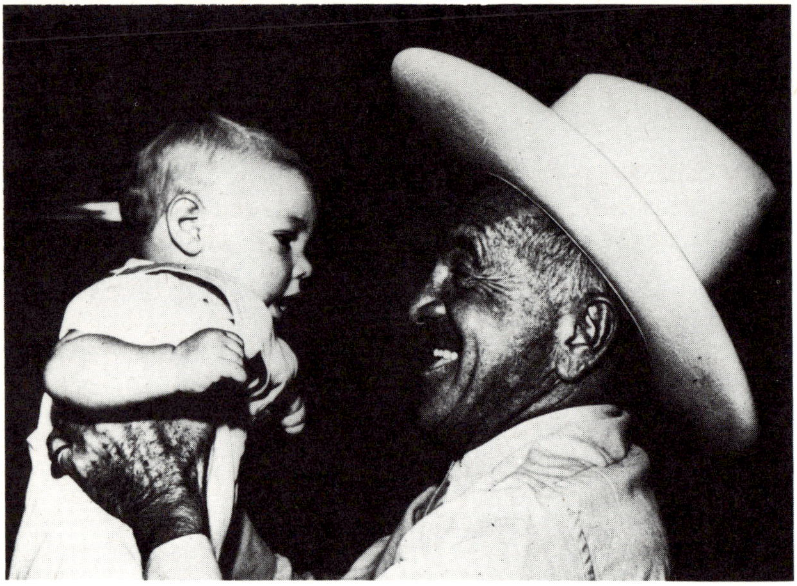

An eyeball-to-eyeball confrontation between Al and Asa, his son, taken in 1949.

Young Arthur MacArthur and his governess joined them, and, when Al learnt that the little boy had seen the Parks-Jolson films, he asked him which songs he had liked best. 'Sonny Boy' was his answer, so Al took him to the big, shiny grand piano and started to sing the song to him. Halfway through the song Al stopped, General MacArthur had come into the room. There were hellos and handshakes all round and the General apologised for barging in during a song. Al forgave him and asked the General to name his own favourite songs. The General said that they all were, and Al needed no prompting: this was his meat and drink. Harry Akst went to the piano, Al leaned against the polished mahogany and, for the next twenty minutes, gave one of the performances of his life.

In the afternoon Al and Harry went on a last-minute shopping expedition, and Al bought two beautiful strings of pearls, one for Erle and one for Harry's wife. Later that evening, they were sitting in the cocktail lounge of the hotel when a military policeman came up to their table with two large envelopes, one for each of them.

Eager as a child on Christmas morning, Al opened his envelope and proudly showed Harry the contents. Inside was an autographed etching of General MacArthur, bearing the inscription: 'To Al Jolson with gratitude and admiration. Douglas MacArthur, Japan, 1950'. With it, in a little plastic jewel box, was a medallion, one side of which bore the words: 'To Al Jolson from Special Services in appreciation of enter-

Al Jolson rides again – on the shoulders of a delighted crowd gathered to welcome him to Chicago during his 1949 publicity tour for *Jolson Sings Again.*

PRESENTING
A CENTURY OF RAILROAD PROGRESS
ADMISSION 25¢
HICAGO WELCOMES

tainment of Armed Forces Personnel – Far East Command'. On the other side was recorded their entire itinerary. Harry Akst's envelope contained the same treasures. That night, Brigadier-General Paul B. Kelly gave a surprise dinner for Al and Harry. During the party they were entertained by a group of geisha girls who amazed Al by singing 'April Showers', 'Dinah' and 'You Are My Sunshine'.

Next morning they took off from Haneda Airport en route for the States and home. Harry by now was worried about Al, who looked ill and was far more exhausted than he realised. He kept asking Harry how he looked. Harry tried to buck him up, and told him that all he needed was a few days in the sun at Palm Springs. Every hour that took them nearer California eased Harry's mind about Al. They landed at Los Angeles Airport on the night of 23 September 1950 to find the press waiting for them. Newsreels ground, flash bulbs popped and Al dropped to his knees and kissed the soil. He was home. A reporter asked him how he felt to be be back in the United States and he replied that he never knew until he checked his

Jolson sings again was certainly the message of the Loew's Theatre Tour which Al undertook in 1949 to publicise the second film biography.

income-tax returns to see if he had paid enough! After this tumultuous reception, which typified people's reaction to him after he returned, an exhausted Al left the airport with Erle having promised to see Harry the next day.

A few days after Al and Harry Akst returned from Korea, Al called Harry to tell him of an offer he had just received from Jerry Wald and Norman Krasna, the new film-producing combine at R.K.O. They proposed that Al should make a picture about the Services Entertainment Organisation, with Jolson, of course, playing himself. Al was wildly excited. He met Harry for lunch and told him that he had a guest show coming up with Crosby in San Francisco, and that after that he would go back to Palm Springs for seven or eight weeks. He went on to say that R.K.O. were going to spend three million dollars on the picture and that they were offering him the largest sum of money he had ever received in his life.

It is widely believed that Al was also contemplating another film proposal after his return from Korea. This was for yet another biographical film, on the same lines as the two Jolson

Miss Chicago welcomes Al Jolson with the kind of tub-thumping, trumpet-sounding parade that Al loved, provided he was part of it.

stories, again to be produced by Harry Cohn and again to be played by Larry Parks. There is ample evidence to suggest that Al would have been reluctant to cooperate on a third Jolson story, and none for believing that he gave serious thought to any such proposal, if, indeed he received one at all.

After dinner, on the night of 17 October, Harry picked up Al from his mother-in-law's house and took him to the prize fight at Olympic Stadium. During the main event, Al complained of indigestion and on the way home called on one of his physicians. The doctor took a cardiograph straight away and told Al that there was a distinct change for the worse. Al did not like this diagnosis and, the following day, went to another doctor who, not wanting to worry him unduly, pointed out that it was the same heart that had been okayed for a million dollars worth of insurance. Al was satisfied. However, as Al was leaving for San Francisco straight away, the doctor recommended a heart specialist there by the name of Dr William Kerr.

This 63-year old is plainly having a high old time. This picture shows what joy Al got out of simply being up on a stage in front of an audience.

On the morning of Monday 23 October, Al called Harry at home, and asked if he was ready to leave. (This was Al's way of saying that he wanted Harry to accompany him on the trip.) They took the two o'clock flight from Los Angeles together. With them went Martin Fried, who was to work on the orchestration. On arrival in San Francisco, they booked into the St Francis Hotel and Al called Bill Morrow, Bing Crosby's writer and producer, to discuss the show that he was going to record with Bing the following day.

Al and Harry Akst left the hotel at about seven o'clock and went to dine at Tarantino's, a fine sea-food restaurant. The place was crowded but, as always, there was a table for Jolie. During the meal, people kept coming over to congratulate Al on the great work he had done for the GIs. This pleased him enormously and he was further delighted when, as they rose to go, everyone in the restaurant stood up, too, to cheer and applaud. Al turned and blew them all a kiss – his last public curtain-call.

Back at the hotel, they discovered Martin Fried at the desk. Al suggested that the three of them should go upstairs and play gin-rummy. Harry declined and, leaving Al and Martin, went next door to finish a song-parody which he was writing. Al and Martin played cards for a while until Al, saying that he would have to take a rest, asked Martin to go downstairs for some bicarbonate of soda. When Martin Fried left, Harry

An exhausted Al arrives with Harry Akst at Tokyo in September 1950 after a harrowing flight.

LCOME
JOLSO

Al – in the driving seat, where he liked to be – arrives at Miryang to perform for patients in the US 8th Army Hospital.

Akst went into the bedroom to find Jolie lying on the bed, thumbing idly through a magazine.

When he saw Harry, Al beat his chest with a stiff finger, said he had a little indigestion and bemoaned the fact that he had departed from his lamb-chop diet. Harry told him that the bicarbonate would relieve his indigestion, but Al was not convinced and asked Harry to call a doctor. Since he had been through many false alarms with Al, Harry was not worried by this. He phoned downstairs for the hotel physician, only to be told that, although there were two of them, they were both on call at the time. Harry relayed the message to Al, who then asked him to look up Dr Kerr and ask him to come over. This Harry did, and Dr Kerr said that he would be finished with what he was doing in half an hour and would come over then. He told Harry to get the house doctor in the meantime. Al was visibly relieved at the news that Dr Kerr would be arriving in so short a time.

Martin Fried arrived with the bicarbonate and, after Harry had prepared it, Al gulped it down. The mixture did not, however, seem to give him any relief, and he told Harry, in a quiet voice, that he did not think he was going to last. This frightened Harry, and he now noticed that Al had been taking his own pulse. He told Al that a bout of indigestion, which was bound to pass, didn't merit such idle talk.

At this point, the hotel nurse walked in. Upon Al telling her that he thought he had no pulse, she took his wrist and felt it, at the same time rubbing his back with her other hand. She told him, reassuringly, that he had a pulse like a baby's.

Al strikes a familiar pose in unfamiliar surroundings at a performance in Pusan Stadium, Korea in September 1950.

All this time, Martin Fried was in the living room arranging the musical layout for the next day's broadcast. To him, too, Al's illness was just another of many false alarms.

At about ten o'clock, the house physician, Dr Walter Beckh, and the heart specialist Dr William Kerr arrived together. They asked a few questions and briefly examined Al who seemed to be somewhat better and disposed to talk. Telling them to draw up a couple of chairs and sit down, which they did, he enquired which of the two was Dr Kerr. Al started to say that he must be a pretty important guy and Dr Kerr agreed that of course he was, apparently thinking that Al meant that he, Al, must be important to rouse him, Dr Kerr, at such a late hour. However, Al proceeded to say, with a smile, that he felt he was important because his interview with MacArthur had lasted two hours, whereas Truman's had only lasted one hour.

Suddenly, without warning, Al reached for his pulse and seemed to be trying to raise himself up from the pillows. Everyone looked at him as he sighed and said, 'I'm going', then sank back again. His eyes closed. Harry Akst gasped, the doctors jumped to their feet and Dr Beckh applied a stethoscope to Al's heart. He then turned to Dr Kerr and confirmed that Al Jolson had died.

Dr Kerr had the unpleasant duty of breaking the news to Jolson's wife, Erle, who was at their home in Encino, California. There was no way to soften the blow for her. She and Al had had only five short, but happy, years of marriage. Thanks to Erle, his homecomings had been worthwhile and the words of his song 'I Want A Girl' had, at last, come true for him.

On 23 October 1950, exactly one month to the day after the plane bearing him from Japan touched down in Los Angeles, Al Jolson died. A black cloud suddenly darkened every continent in which he had performed. The same shadow was cast over the front page of newspapers in every land. Entire front pages of major American Newspapers were devoted to the event. Massive banner headlines sounded the general grief from newstands everywhere, some of these headlines even standing above the names of the newspapers themselves.

Al Jolson's funeral was one of the biggest that New York has ever seen. His public were turned away in their thousands as his body lay in state at the Temple Israel, the venue for his

Al, tragically, tops the bill for the last time; the death of this most American of Americans is recorded amid the first stirrings of 'McCarthy mania'.

AN AMERICAN PAPER FOR AMERICANS

Chicago Daily Tribune

THE WORLD'S GREATEST NEWSPAPER

Founded June 10, 1847

64 PAGES ★★★ SPORTS FINAL

VOLUME CIX—NO. 254 TUESDAY, OCTOBER 24, 1950 FOUR CENTS—PAY NO MORE

JOLSON DIES PLAYING CARDS

FBI Jails 20 Reds in Roundup; 3 Seized in Chicago

CHURCH FIRE INJURES FIVE; $500,000 LOSS

1,400 Pupils Quit School

NEWS SUMMARY OF THE TRIBUNE

STAR STRICKEN IN HOTEL ROOM ON WEST COAST

64, He Was Back from Korea

DOING HIS WORK FOR HIM

RESERVE TO GET 5 MONTH NOTICE

Order Will Affect All Services

North Shore Ready for Brave Show of U. N. Flags Today

Sportsman's Suspended in Wake of Quiz

U. S. MARKS 86 FOR ARREST AS SOVIET AGENTS

Aliens in 11 Cities Held by Raiders

CUTTER SAVES 8 OF 20 ABOARD MISSING FRATER

THE WEATHER

2d Expected Baby Lost by Lana Turner in Fall

Extra Charge Gives Bang to 131st Infantry Fete

HAVE YOU Registered Your Name IN THE TRIBUNE'S New Offer? YOU CAN GET A GIFT WITHOUT COST! See Page 2, Part 2

FOR SEPTEMBER, 1950 DAILY 940,000 THE CHICAGO TRIBUNE

last full house. On that October day in 1950, the man finally stepped down, and the legend, his patient understudy which had been growing with him through the years, took over the part. Today, Al Jolson, the legend, is still taking the curtain-calls which his adoring public have constantly begged down the years.

Tributes

Al Jolson had held the stage, more or less unchallenged, for more than three decades. With his death he again, for the last time, made the headlines. This would have pleased him. Jolson loved the theatre, he loved being on stage, he loved to see the faces when he sang. Jolson also loved Jolson the entertainer, and loved his success. He, it must be admitted, was egocentric to a degree. It was because of the way he was that we had the Jolson everybody knew and loved. His death unleashed tribute from all over the world. What follows is but a small stream diverted from the general flood.

The first and most moving of these tributes to *the* Jazz Singer comes from the obituary written by George Jessel, the other Jazz Singer.

THE MAJESTY OF JOLIE

BY

George Jessel

A breeze from San Francisco Bay, and the life of the greatest minstrel America has ever known is in the balance. A turn of a card – telling of a gag – and within a few moments, a wife, a legion of friends, and a nation are broken-hearted. So it was – and so, alas, it is – the passing from this earthly scene of Al Jolson. And the voice that put majesty into the American popular song must from now on come from a disc instead of the heart, from whence it came.

It will take a long time for the people in my business who have been wounded by his death to become reconciled that this dynamic bundle of energy with its God-given talent that called itself Al Jolson, is at peace. The very humanly emotional heart of the theatrical business does not heal so easily, and the tears that must fall from the eyes of the many who miss him already cannot be halted by the spoken word. No, the word will not take the place of his song.

And not only has the entertainment world lost its king, but we cannot cry, 'The King is dead – long live the King!' for there is no one to hold his sceptre. Those of us who tarry behind are but pale imitations, mere princelings.

American Jewry suffers as well – and I must inform you of the great inspiration that Al was to the Jewish people in the last forty years. For in 1910 the Jewish people who emigrated from Europe to come here were a sad lot. Their humor came out of their own troubles. Men of thirty-five seemed to take on the attitude of their fathers and grandfathers – they walked with stooped shoulders. When they sang, they sang with lament in their hearts and their voices, always as if they were pleading for help from above. And the actors,

Erle Galbraith Jolson with Secretary of Defense Marshall and Asa, at the Pentagon on 6 December 1950 after Asa had received Al's posthumous Medal of Merit. The citation stated that 'his contribution to the United Nations action in Korea was made at the expense of his life . . . '

even the great ones, came on the stage also playing characters like their fathers. Vaudeville, the musical comedy stage and the legitimate theatre had Ben Welch and Joe Welch, monologists with beards and shabby clothes telling humorous stories that had a tear behind them. Likewise did this happen in legitimate theatre: David Warfield in *The Auctioneer*, *The Music Master*, and many others, in plays bewailing the misfortunes that had happened to the Jew.

Then there came on the scene a young man, vibrantly pulsing life and courage, who marched on the stage, head high with the authority of a Roman emperor, with a gaiety that was militant, uninhibited and unafraid, and told the world that the Jew in America did not only have to sing in sorrow, but could shout happily about Dixie, about the Night Boat to Albany, about coming to California, about a Girl in Avalon. And when he cried 'Mammy', it was in appreciation, not in lament.

Jolson is the happiest portrait that can ever be painted about an

This magnificent memorial dominates the highway approach to Hollywood in remembrance of the man who, amongst many, many other achievements, brought the talkie to town.

American of the Jewish faith. Jolson was synonymous with victory – at the race track, at the ball game, at anything that he participated in, he would say, 'I had the winner, ha, ha, why didn't you ask me?' This was not in bravado alone – this was the quintessence of optimism. Whatever you're in, whatever game you play, feel like you are the winner.

The history of the world does not say enough about how important the song and the singer have been. But history must record the name Jolson, who in the twilight of his life sang his heart out in a foreign land, to the wounded and to the valiant. I am proud to have basked in the sunlight of his greatness, to have been part of his time. . . .

The tribute by George Jessel was typical of the heart-rending and moving reaction of the world's press to the shock of Al's death. Radio was no slower to record its grief and register its praise. Soon after Al's passing, the B.B.C. presented a programme entitled *Jolson Sings On*, in which the part of Al was played by a British entertainer, Max Bygraves. Whatever merits Mr Bygraves may have as a contemporary performer, it was obvious that he was dwarfed by Al's songs and reputation.

On the very evening of Al's death, radio stations all over the world were paying tributes. I have at least 150 hours of tape featuring the other greats, including Bob Hope, Cantor and Jessel paying their sincere tributes both at the time of his death and later. What follows is one of the finest eulogies delivered then – a eulogy which also serves as one of the finest appreciations and remembrances of Jolie the man and the entertainer.

JOLIE THE KING

BY

Eddie Cantor

I was in Mobile, Alabama, when I first got the shocking news from an N.B.C. official in New York that Al Jolson was dead of a heart attack. The telephone operator who put the call through to me was sobbing hysterically. The elevator operator who took me downstairs couldn't control his tears. The taxi-driver who drove me to the N.B.C. studios to do a special memorial broadcast kept mumbling to himself, 'Why did he have to go?' The attendants and technicians at the studio were all red-eyed from weeping. None of these people had ever met Al Jolson personally. Yet, because Jolie was a man of the people, because he seemed to know and love everyone who had ever heard the sound of his voice, the grief over his passing was universal.

Jolie had human frailties, just as any other man. I say this in all sincerity and with my heart full of love for the man we all knew as 'The King'. Jollie's great heart, his wonderful almost childlike spirit, and his overflowing love of humanity overshadowed everything else. He never forgot his nearness to the people and his nearness to his God. Those of us who kidded him the most, loved him the most. Whenever the gang – Jack Benny, George Jessel, George Burns and Jolie – used to gather at my house, there was never a night when we didn't get together to sing 'Mammy'. But there was never anybody who could sing 'Mammy' like Jolson could.

We all looked upon him with envy because we could never hope to reach his stature, but he was also an inspiration to all his contemporaries. He was six acts of top billing rolled into one, and for anyone

A man already in the shadow of his legend, Al posed for this picture in 1947.

to compete with him was like watching a midget in a sideshow trying to touch the giant's head. To call him the biggest hunk of entertainer in show business was an understatement. He was the only entertainer who was his own lighting and his own scenery.

Jolie always loved to play jokes and get a laugh. I remember one time when I was playing opposite him in Chicago. We both lived in the Belmont Hotel in Chicago's North Side, and we used to meet after our shows and kid each other and lie to one another about the take at the box office that night. We spent hours with each other every night for five months and I never had so much fun in all my life. The newspapers kept trying to cook up a phony feud between us but neither one of us took it seriously. Then, one day, I came down with pleurisy and my doctor advised me to close my show and take a rest.

'I can't Doc,' I told him, 'then all the newspapers will say, "Jolson drives Cantor out of town".'

Sick as I was, I kept going night after night. But then finally, I got so weak I couldn't even walk out on the stage and so I closed the show and left for New York. Imagine my amazement when I got off the train, picked up the *New York Times* and read this headline on the theatrical page: 'Jolson closes his show immediately after Cantor closes his show.' It turned out that Jolie had been sicker than I was, but he'd kept going only because he didn't want the newspapers to say: 'Cantor drives Jolson out of town.'

Jolie brought joy to more people than any other man alive. He was more than an actor or a singer or an entertainer – he was an experience. We kidded him about his age but he was ageless. I still cannot believe and refuse to accept the fact that he is gone. He has left his footprints on the sands of time, and he will be alive to all of us, just as long as we can turn on a record and hear his God-given voice that never fails to bring a strangely comforting catch in the throat and a feeling of goodness to the heart.

The following sentiments are credited to Larry Parks. However his moving, if florid, tribute only goes to show that newspapers can and do rearrange the facts, and that not every funeral knell rings wholly with truth. Larry Parks undoubtedly loved and respected Al, but he is also on record more than once as saying that their smooth relationship was occasionally ruffled by Al's jealousy.

Jolson was big. He was a dynamic bundle of energy, and it often seemed as if his voice was just an outlet – though a rare outlet, to be sure – for his amazing vitality and endurance.

He was a man of strong physical fibre, sparked by his talent, and his boundless yearning to share it with all. And it was this, and his sheer will to live and to be with his fellows, that sustained him through a devastating illness, which resulted from his insistence on entertaining troops in North Africa in World War II.

That it would not sustain him through the aftermath of his trip to Korea is probably something he never considered. Or, if he did face the problem, it was probably with the desire and willingness to take his last curtain-call where it could do the most good for hearts not as tired as his.

Though I made two pictures truly in his shadow, I never really knew Jolson well. I did and I didn't. He was encouraging, inspiring, a challenge to every ounce of talent for entertaining and acting that I may possess. He illuminated and magnetized everything he did.

Stepping into his shoes was, for me, a matter of endless study, observation, energetic concentration to obtain, perfectly if possible, a simulation of the kind of man he was.

It is not surprising, therefore, that whilst making *The Jolson Story* I spent 107 days before the cameras and lost eighteen pounds in weight.

We worked hard together, and as he wanted me to be Jolson on film as much as I wanted to be, he was invariably delighted and enthusiastic when he felt I had captured the 'Jolie' audiences knew.

And then from nowhere, due to vagaries that creep into columns from sources unknown, came reports that we were feuding, reports which persisted for some time until they ultimately fell of their own weight. They were untrue, Jolson and I were enthusiastic co-workers, with a sound regard for one another. There was never a disagreement between us.

I confess that, at the outset, I had no desire to be Jolson but that was certainly not through any lack of admiration, I simply felt that I was not the one to do the role justice. It is surprising now, that the studio chiefs were even interested in an actor who was not brash enough to say he could at least perform a silent mimicry of the Mammy Singer. But they were. In fact, they became so insistent on a test, that I plunged into research.

Friends helped me dig up some of Al's early films, and I ran them over and over again in a projection room. I haunted music stores around Los Angeles to acquire old Jolson records, which I played by the hour. What I was trying to get was the beat, the tempo, and the swing that Jolie had, that ability to make audiences share his very pulse beat.

By the time the actual test came, I was probably the best informed man on Jolson then in circulation.

And I must have caught some of the spark, because it was Jolie who finally okayed me.

Very early in the preparations for *The Jolson Story*, Al showed me how to mime to his songs. 'You move around too much kid,' he said, 'I'll show you.' We were in my dressing room when he began his demonstration of the 'easy' Jolson manner. When he finished just one number, the lamps and furnishings, not to speak of his audience, looked as if they had been in a hurricane.

It was then that Jolie turned to me with a broad smile. 'See, kid?' he said, 'you gotta take it easy.' On another occasion, in the midst of rehearsals, he asked me if I'd noticed the way he always timed a certain gesture to the music of the theatre orchestra. Embarrassed, I had to confess I'd never seen him on stage. 'Son, you ain't seen nothin' yet,' he kidded, reaching for a phone. He arranged for an orchestra to be sent into a theatre that had been built on an adjoining stage. Half an hour later, I became the only person in the world to sit in solitary grandeur and have a full Al Jolson show put on for my sole benefit.

But it mattered little to him whether he was playing to an audience of millions over the radio or to a tiny gathering of three or four Servicemen or civilians. He invariably gave his best, and how he loved to see the pleasure he brought people.

Only a handful of Americans, I believe, have ever done more to promote goodwill and understanding amongst Protestants, Catholics and Jews. And Al did it with songs and laughs.

'All you need is tolerance,' he told his friends, 'and understanding.' And the best way to promote that is by something truly universal – music and laughter. That's a language everybody appreciates.

That was one of his primary motives in allowing *The Jolson Story* and later *Jolson Sings Again* to come to the screen. Motion pictures, he always believed, were ideally suited for spreading kindness around the world.

'You sing to people and get them into the right mood, and presently they become aware of something, almost unconsciously, they realise that they're all pretty much alike,' he said. I'm afraid it's going to be a long time before any of us will see the like of this outstanding troubadour again. He represented an age, an era, a tradition in show business, that there are few to carry on.

It was a personal sort of appeal he had that endeared him to all types of audiences. More than any other entertainer of our generation, Jolson has already become a legend.

I remember a few years ago when a group of us went up to Santa Barbara to see a sneak preview of the first Jolson picture. Al was standing in the lobby listening to the comments as the audience left the theatre. A woman said, 'It's too bad Jolson isn't alive to see it.' For, even then, Jolson had become such a towering individual, a landmark in show business history, that, to many, it hardly seemed possible that he could still be alive.

To crown the catafalque of praise that a multitude of people and organisations immediately erected by their individual

'The man raised on high, the sweet singer of Isarael' is commemorated in bronze in Los Angeles.

offerings, came a unique tribute from the nation he loved so dearly, and for whose fighting men he gave so much. On 6 December 1950, the Medal of Merit was posthumously awarded to Al Jolson by President Truman. At the request of Al's widow, Erle, to whom the medal was presented, it was pinned on the chest of his three-year-old son, Asa. The wheel had come full circle. The United States of America, to which young Asa Yeolson had come so quietly four decades earlier, was showing fitting gratitude to his even more youthful namesake.

The final and most lasting memorial to Al Jolson was left by his wife. It stands in a cemetery in the Los Angeles that had seen so many of his comings and goings. The late Jack Benny, one of Al's friends from the old days (who now lies beside Al), described it as: 'a monument of unmatched beauty, erected to the world's greatest entertainer.'

Standing high above the highway into Hollywood, it has four white marble columns thirty-five feet tall, and a mosaic ceiling under it's dome depicting the mighty Moses with the tablets of the Commandments. Encircling the dome reads the gilt inscription: 'the man raised on high, the sweet singer of Israel.' Beneath, the bronze statue of 'the Mammy Singer' kneels in a hauntingly familiar attitude more eloquent than a thousand tributes.

Epilogue

Just as Al Jolson was the only man who could supply this book with a proper opening, so now, as the latest act in his legend draws to a close, he is the only man who could fitly speak its closing words.

His pal Harry Akst, standing, not long after Al's death, in a New York hotel suite they often shared, recalled the time when he had tried in vain to call Al's attention to a band parading below on Fifth Avenue. Al's indifference provoked Harry to ask him if if he disliked parades. Al replied that he loved a parade – so long as it didn't pass him by.

During his life, Al Jolson never let the parade pass him by. Even now, after his death, he is still in front showing the rest of us the way. He steps out in many guises. His films still delight television viewers in the U.S.A. and Britain. In recent years, the B.B.C. showed *The Jolson Story* on Christmas Day – to spectacular acclaim – and followed it with *Jolson Sings Again* on New Year's Day, fitting occasions, both of them, for releasing once more those bubbling, rich, life-loving tones. In 1970, Columbia's 70mm remake of *The Jolson Story* was unveiled to an ecstatic, celebrity-packed audience.

Sales of his recordings continue unabated, and complete Jolson albums are much sought after. Even the first recordings, dating from as early as 1924, but now reprocessed with miraculously good results, are tremendously popular. For those of us who wish to enjoy Al's music, as he would have wished us to, in a collected audience, the International Al Jolson Society, the biggest fan club in the world, provides a living focus on the man and his music. Yes, Al Jolson is still there, where he always, out front.

For all those who saw him perform, life seemed brighter, people seemed happier – the world seemed somehow a more hopeful place. Al Jolson, the man with the rainbow round his shoulder, revealed the beauty of life simply by showing his own love for it. Hugging the world to him, he sang – to make laughter, to beguile sadness, to foil despair, and to foster hope. All his life, Al Jolson sang for love.

The World's Greatest Entertainer may no longer sing for us in person, but his undying legacy, the incomparable voice, daily enriches our lives, defying the passage of the years.

And the world to which he gave so much? It will always love and listen to the unforgettable, irresistable man who asked of it only one favour in return:

Let me sing and I'm happy

Al Jolson's Recordings: An Index

When Al Jolson was travelling in vaudeville, the only way to reach an audience was to go to them. Thirty years later, the push button had replaced the rail ticket and the only way that most artists travelled was by radio wave or gramophone stylus. The living song of the minstrel was gradually lost in the blare of the loudspeaker, and, as live performers had less and less 'say' in the world of entertainment, so it was that the microphone did more and more of the talking.

Even if he did so with a wistful backward glance, Al, like all great men, accepted that he had to move with the times, and, from the first, took every opportunity of making records. Before the twenties had traversed half their giddy span, Al had dozens of his songs on wax.

The result of this pioneering spirit is a huge library of recordings, which, sadly, cannot be fully catalogued here. So what follows is only an alphabetical listing of his more memorable numbers. For the complete list of Jolson records, the reader will have to turn to that exhaustive compendium of Alstatistics – *Jolsongraphy*.

In the following index all record company labels given are those of the original issue only. Re-issues, both domestic and foreign, are not given. Whenever a song has been recorded more than once by Al, its title is listed once for each original label release, chronologically by recording date. One asterisk (*) indicates a selection taken from a radio broadcast. Two asterisks (**) refer to a hitherto unreleased recording.

Al's contractual periods with the recording companies were

as follows: Victor 1911–3; Columbia 1913–23; Brunswick 1924–32; V-Disc 1943–7; Decca 1945–50.

The single song for the Souvenir label was a private recording for Al's brother Harry in 1938.

A

About a Quarter to Nine	Decca
After You've Gone	Decca
Alabamy Bound*	Decca
Alexander's Ragtime Band (w. Bing Crosby)	Decca
Alexander's Ragtime Band* (w. Bing Crosby)	V-Disc
Alexander's Ragtime Band*	Decca
All Alone	Brunswick
All Alone* (w. Oscar Levant, piano)	Decca
All By Myself* (w. Bing Crosby)	V-Disc
All By Myself*	Decca
All My Love	Decca
Almost Like Being in Love*	Decca
Always*	Decca
Among My Souvenirs*	Decca
And Mimi*	Decca
Angel Child	Columbia
Annie Laurie*	Decca
Anniversary Song	Decca
Anniversary Song* (w. Oscar Levant, piano)	Decca
April Showers	Columbia
April Showers	Brunswick
April Showers	Decca
April Showers	V-Disc
Arcady	Columbia
Are You Lonesome Tonight?	Decca
Asleep in the Deep-Parody	Victor
At Peace With the World	Brunswick
At Sundown*	Decca
At the Candlelight Cafe* (w. Oscar Levant, piano)	Decca
Avalon	Columbia
Avalon	Decca

B

Baby Face*	Decca
Baby Face (Medley: 'Jolson Sings Again')	Decca
Back in Your Own Backyard	Brunswick

Back in Your Own Backyard	Decca
Back to the Carolina You Love	Columbia
Back to the Carolina You Love	Little Wonder
Beautiful Dreamer	Decca
Best Things in Life Are Free, The*	Decca
Blue River	Brunswick
Brass Band Ephraham Jones	Victor
Bright Eyes*	Decca
Broken Doll, A	Columbia
By the Light of the Silvery Moon	Decca

C

California, Here I Come (w. Buddy DeSylva, uke)	Brunswick
California, Here I Come	Decca
Cantor, The (Sung in Yiddish)	Decca
Carolina in the Morning	Decca
Chinatown, My Chinatown*	Decca
Chinatown, My Chinatown	Decca
Chicago*	Decca
Chloe	Columbia
Coal-Black Mammy	Columbia
Come to Me, Bend to Me*	Decca
Coo-Coo	Columbia

D

De Camptown Races	Decca
Dinah*	Decca
Ding-a-Ring a Ring	Columbia
Dirty Hands! Dirty Face!	Brunswick
Dirty Hands! Dirty Face!* (w. Oscar Levant, piano)	Decca
Do I (Do I-Do I Love Her?)**	Columbia
Don't Forget the Boys (Who Fought For You and Me)**	Columbia
Don't Let It Get You Down*	Decca
Don't Write Me Letters	Columbia
Down Among the Sheltering Palms (w. Mills Bros.)	Decca
Down By the Ohio – See: O-Hi-O (O-My-O!)	Columbia

Down Where the Swanee River Flows	Columbia
Du Host A Liebes Punim – See: You Have a Lovely Face	Souvenir

E

Easter Parade* (w. Bing Crosby)	V-Disc
Easter Parade*	Decca
Eeeny Meany Miney Moe**	Columbia
Everybody Snap Your Fingers With Me	Columbia
Ev'ry Little While	Columbia

F

Feeling the Way I Do	Brunswick
Fellow Needs a Girl, A*	Decca
Follow the Swallow	Brunswick
For Me and My Gal	Decca
For Me and My Gal*	Decca
Four Walls	Brunswick
From Here to Shanghai	Columbia

G

Give Me My Mammy	Columbia
Give My Regards to Broadway	Decca
God's Country	Decca
Golden Gate	Brunswick
Golden Gate	Decca

H

Hallelujah, I'm a Bum	Brunswick
Hannah in Savannah*	Decca
Hatikvoh (National Anthem of Israel) (sung in Hebrew)	Decca
Hello, Central, Give Me No Man's Land	Columbia
Hello, 'Tucky (w. Buddy DeSylva, uke)	Brunswick
Hello, 'Tucky*	Decca
Her Danny**	Columbia
Here I Am	Brunswick

Home In Pasadena | Brunswick

Home In Pasadena	Brunswick
Hot Time In the Old Town Tonight, A* (w. Oscar Levant, piano)	Decca
How Deep Is the Ocean?*	Decca

I

I Can't Give You Anything But Love* (w. Oscar Levant, piano)	Decca
I'd Climb the Highest Mountain – See: If I Knew I'd Find You	Brunswick
I Dream of Jeanie With the Light Brown Brown Hair	Decca

If I Knew I'd Find You – See: I'd Climb the Highest Mountain	Brunswick
If I Only Had a Match	Decca
If We Can't Be the Same Old Sweethearts*	Decca
I Gave Her That	Columbia
I Got Lucky In the Rain*	Decca
I'll Be Seeing You*	Decca
I'll Say She Does	Columbia
I'll See You In My Dreams*	Decca
I'll Stand Beneath Your Window Tonight and Whistle	Columbia
I Love You (Just One Way to Say)	Decca
I'm All Bound 'Round With the Mason Dixon Line	Columbia
I'm Always Chasing Rainbows*	Decca
I'm Always Chasing Rainbows* (w. Oscar Levant, piano)	Decca
I'm Crying Just For You	Decca
I'm Down in Honolulu Looking Them Over	Columbia
I'm Goin' South	Columbia
I'm Goin' South	Brunswick
I'm Gonna Tramp, Tramp, Tramp	Brunswick
I'm In Seventh Heaven	Brunswick
I'm Just Wild About Harry	Decca
I'm Looking Over a Four Leaf Clover (Medley: 'Jolson Sings Again)	Decca
I'm Saving Up the Means to Get to New Orleans	Columbia
I'm Sitting On Top of the World	Brunswick
I'm Sitting On Top of the World	Decca
In Our House	Decca
In Sweet September	Columbia
In the Good Old Summertime* (w. Oscar Levant, piano)	Decca
I Only Have Eyes For You	Decca
I Sent My Wife to the Thousand Isles	Columbia
Is It True What They Say About Dixie? (w. Mills Bros.)	Decca
Is It True What They Say About Dixie?	Decca
Israel	Decca

It Ain't Necessarily So* (w. Oscar Levant, piano)	Decca
It All Depends On You	Decca
I've Got My Captain Working For Me Now	Columbia
I've Gotta Get Back to New York*	Decca
I Want a Girl Just Like the Girl That Married Dear Old Dad	Decca
I Wish I Had a Girl	Decca
I Wish I Had My Old Gal Back Again	Brunswick
I Wonder What's Become of Sally	Brunswick
I Wonder What's Become of Sally*	Decca
I Wonder Why She Kept On Saying 'Si-Si-Si-Si Signor'	Columbia

J

Just One of Those Things*	Decca

K

(Keep Smiling at Trouble) Trouble's a Bubble	Brunswick
(Trouble's a Bubble) Keep Smiling at Trouble	Decca
Kol Nidre (sung in Aramaic)	Decca

L

Lazy	Brunswick
Lazy*	V-Disc
Let Me Sing and I'm Happy	Brunswick
Let Me Sing and I'm Happy	Decca
Let's Go West Again	Decca
Little Girl*	Decca
Little Pal	Brunswick
Little Pal*	Decca
Liza (All the Clouds'll Roll Away)	Brunswick
Liza (All the Clouds'll Roll Away)	Decca
Look For the Silver Lining*	Decca
Looking at You (Across the Breakfast Table)	Brunswick
Lost (A Wonderful Girl)	Columbia

M

Ma Blushin' Rosie (Ma Posie Sweet)	V-Disc
Ma Blushin' Rosie (Ma Posie Sweet)	Decca
Ma Blushin' Rosie (Ma Posie Sweet)*	Decca
Ma (He's Making Eyes At Me)*	Decca
Mamma Loves Papa**	Columbia
Mandalay	Brunswick
Marcheta (A Love Song of Old Mexico)*	Decca
Margie*	Decca
Mary's a Grand Old Name* (w. Oscar Levant, piano)	Decca

Massa's in De Cold, Cold Ground	Decca
Maxim's* (w. Oscar Levant, piano)	Decca
Memories*	Decca
Miami	Brunswick
Mr Radio Man	Brunswick
Morning Will Come	Columbia
Mother of Mine, I Still Have You	Brunswick
Movin' Man, Don't Take My Baby Grand!	Victor
My Blue Heaven*	Decca
My Gal Sal*	Decca
My Mammy	Brunswick
My Mammy	Decca
My Mammy*	V-Disc
My Melancholy Baby*	Decca
My Mother's Rosary	Decca
My Old Kentucky Home	Decca
My Papa Doesn't Two-Time No Time	Brunswick
My Sumurun Girl**	Victor
My Yellow Jacket Girl	Victor

N

Nearest Thing to Heaven*	Decca
Near You*	Decca
Never Again	Brunswick
'N' Everything	Columbia
No Sad Songs For Me	Decca
Now He's Got a Beautiful Girl	Columbia

O

Oh, How I Miss You Tonight* (w. Oscar Levant, piano)	Decca
O-HI-O (O-My!-O!) – See: Down By the Ohio	Columbia
Oh! Susanna	Decca
Oh, You Beautiful Doll* (w. Red Nichols, trumpet)	Decca
Old Black Joe	Decca
Old Folks at Home (Swanee River)	Decca
Ol' Man River	Brunswick

Ol' Man River*	Decca
Old Piano Roll Blues, The (w. Andrews Sisters)	Decca
One I Love Belongs to Somebody Else, The	Brunswick
One I Love Belongs to Somebody Else, The* (w. Bing Crosby)	V-Disc
One I Love Belongs to Somebody Else, The* (w. Oscar Levant, piano)	Decca
One I Love Belongs to Somebody Else, The*	Decca
One Sweet Kiss (Mem'ries of)	Brunswick
On the Road to Calais	Columbia
Oogie Oogie Wa Wa	Columbia

P

Paris Wakes and Smiles	Decca
Peg O' My Heart*	Decca
Poor Butterfly* (w. Oscar Levant, piano)	Decca
Pray For Sunshine (But Always Be Prepared For Rain)	Columbia
Pretty Baby	Decca
Pullman Porters On Parade	Columbia

R

Ragging the Baby To Sleep	Victor
Ramona* (w. Oscar Levant, piano)	Decca
Real Piano Player, A* (w. Jimmy Durante)	Decca
Remember (You Forgot to)	Brunswick
Remember (You Forgot to)*	Decca
Remember Mother's Day*	Decca
Remember Mother's Day	Decca
Revival Day	Columbia
Rock-a-Bye Your Baby With a Dixie Melody	Columbia
Rock-a-Bye Your Baby With a Dixie Melody	Brunswick
Rock-a-Bye Your Baby With a Dixie Melody	Decca
Rock-a-Bye Your Baby With a Dixie Melody* (w. Oscar Levant, piano)	Decca

Rosalie*	Decca
Roses of Picardy*	Decca
Rum Tum Tiddle	Victor

S

Say It Isn't So*	Decca
Scandinavia (Sing Dose Song and Make Dose Music)	Columbia
Schubert's Serenade* (Oscar Levant, piano)	Decca
She Is My Daisy*	Decca
She Knows It**	Columbia
She's a Latin From Manhattan* (piano-verse only- Oscar Levant,)	Decca
Shine On, Harvest Moon* (w. Oscar Levant, piano)	Decca
Sister Susie's Sewing Shirts For Soldiers	Columbia
Snap Your Fingers	Victor
Some Beautiful Morning (I'll Hold You In My Arms)	Columbia
Some Enchanted Evening	Decca
Some of These Days**	Columbia
Someone Else May Be There While I'm Gone	Columbia
Someone Else May Be There While I'm Gone	Decca
Sonny Boy	Brunswick
Sonny Boy	Decca
Spaniard That Blighted My Life, The	Victor
Spaniard That Blighted My Life, The (w. Bing Crosby)	Decca
Stella	Colombia
Steppin' Out	Columbia
Swanee	Columbia
Swanee	Decca
Swanee*	V-Disc

T

Tell Me (Why Nights Are Lonely)	Columbia
Tell That to the Marines	Columbia
That Big Blonde Mamma	Columbia

That Certain Party*	Decca
That Haunting Melody	Victor
That Little German Band	Columbia
That Lovin' Traumerei	Victor
That Lovin' Traumerei* (w. Oscar Levant, piano)	Decca
That Old Gang Old Mine*	Decca
That Wonderful Girl of Mine	Decca
That Wonderful Kid from Madrid	Columbia
There's a Broken Heart For Every Light On Broadway**	Columbia
There's a Lump of Sugar Down in Dixie	Columbia
There's a Rainbow 'Round My Shoulder	Brunswick

There's a Rainbow 'Round My Shoulder	Decca
Tillie Titwillow	Columbia
Till the End of Time* (w. Oscar Levant, piano)	Decca
To My Mammy	Brunswick
Tonight's My Night With Baby	Brunswick
Toot Toot Tootsie!	Columbia
Toot Toot Tootsie!	Decca
Toot Toot Tootsie!*	Decca
Tree in a Meadow, A	Decca
Twelve O'clock At Night	Columbia

U

Uncle Sammy** (March and Two-Step)	Victor
Used to You	Brunswick

V

Villain Still Pursued Her, The**	Victor

W

Waitin' For the Evening' Mail	Columbia
Waiting For the Robert E. Lee	Decca
Wanita	Columbia
Water Boy* (w. Oscar Levant, piano)	Decca
Way Down Yonder In New Orleans (w. Andrews Sisters)	Decca
Wedding Bells (Will You Ever Ring For Me?)	Columbia
What'll I Do*	Decca
When Day is Done*	Decca
When I Leave the World Behind	Decca
When Irish Eyes Are Smiling* (w. Oscar Levant, piano)	Decca
When the Grown Up Ladies Act Like Babies	Columbia
When the Little Red Roses Get the Blues For You	Brunswick
When the Red Red Robin Comes Bob Bob Bobbin' Along	Brunswick

When the Red Red Robin Comes Bob Bob Bobbin' Along	Decca
When You Were Sweet Sixteen	Decca
When You Were Sweet Sixteen*	Decca
Where Did Robinson Crusoe Go With Friday On Saturday Night?	Columbia
Where Did Robinson Crusoe Go With Friday On Saturday Night?*	Decca
Where the Black-Eyed Susans Grow	Decca
Whispering*	Decca
Who and Where*	Decca
Who Cares?	Columbia
Who Played Poker With Pocahontas?	Columbia
Who Wants a Bad Little Boy?	Brunswick
Why Can't You?	Brunswick
Without a Song*	Decca

Y

Yaaka Hula Hickey Dula	Columbia
Yaaka Hula Hickey Dula*	Decca
Yoo-Hoo	Columbia
You Ain't Nothing Yet	Columbia
You Are Too Beautiful	Brunswick
You Flew Away From the Nest	Brunswick
You Have A Lovely Face – See: Du Host a Liebes Punim	Souvenir
You'll Always Be Beautiful*	Decca
You Made Me Love You	Columbia
You Made Me Love You	Decca
You Made Me Love You*	Decca
You're a Dangerous Girl	Columbia
You've Simply Got Me Cuckoo	Columbia

Al Jolson's Films

1927

AL JOLSON as Jackie Rabinowitz/Jack Robin in

THE JAZZ SINGER

The Players
May McAvoy (Mary Dale), Warner Oland (Cantor Rabinowitz), Eugenie Besserer (Sara Rabinowitz), Otto Lederer (Moisha Yudelson), Himself (Cantor Josef Rosenblatt), Bobbie Gordon (Jackie, at 13 years), Richard Tucker (Harry Lee), Nat Carr (Levi), William Demarest (Buster Billings), Anders Randolf (Billings), Will Walling (Doctor), Myrna Loy (Chorus Girl).

Warner Bros. – Vitaphone. Directed by Alan Crosland. Screenplay by Alfred A. Cohn from the play by Samson Raphaelson (as produced on the stage by Lewis and Gordon and Sam H. Harris). Camera: Hal Mohr. Opened 6 October 1927 at the Warner Theatre in New York. Nine reels.

Al puts a comforting face on things for Eugenie Besserer in *The Jazz Singer*, which had a story uncannily similar to Jolson's own.

The picture that ushered in the age of the talkies had a story which uncannily ressembled that of Al's own life. In the film, as in real life, the hero flies in the face of family tradition by taking to the stage instead of becoming a cantor in the Jewish church, like his father. The film grossed a fortune for Warner Bros. and for Al, who had taken a typical calculated risk in making the film. It also won a 'Special Award' for Warner Bros. in the 1927–8 Academy Award Presentations, which was actually presented to Al.

The *Jazz Singer* included the following songs: 'Dirty Hands, Dirty Face'; 'Toot, Toot, Tootsie Goo'bye', with its whistled second chorus – an ad-lib which Al sprang on his unsuspecting colleagues; 'Blue Skies'; 'Mother Of Mine'; 'I Still Have You' co-authored by Al; 'Kol Nidre', a sacred Jewish chant; and, of course, 'My Mammy', a partnership of singer and song so important that, prior to the revival of the film in the 1950s, the Museum of Modern Art made up a clip of Al singing the song, for historical purposes. Non-singing sequences in the film were acted in pantomime and accompanied by the synchronized music of the Vitaphone Orchestra, with Lou Silvers arranging and conducting a variety of classical excerpts and standard popular songs.

Looking from the inside out, Al is seen leading the band in *The Singing Fool* (1928).

1928

AL JOLSON as Al Stone in

THE SINGING FOOL

The Players
Betty Bronson (Grace Farrel), Josephine Dunn (Molly Winton), Davey Lee (Sonny Boy), Reed Howes (John Perry), Edward Martindel (Marcus), Arthur Houseman (Blackie Joe). R. E. O'Connor (Billie Cline), Helen Lynch (Maid), Agnes Franey (Chorus Girl).

Warner Bros. – Vitaphone. Directed by Lloyd Bacon. Screenplay by C. Graham Baker from an original work by Leslie S. Barrows. Camera: Byron Haskin. Opened 19 September 1928 at the Winter Garden, New York. Eleven reels.

This talkie follow-up was heralded by an 'announcement trailer' in which Al, in blackface, having silenced the canned applause of his entrance by an imperious whistle, urges the audience to see the new film, while thanking them for seeing the previous one. *The Singing Fool* alternated silent pantomime sequences with sound vocal sequences behind which blared a constant background of mood music supplied by the Vitaphone Orchestra. Apart from the songs performed by Al, this music was made up of snatches from at least thirty other popular songs and eight themes: 'The Streets of New York'; 'My Mammy'; 'Rockabye Your Baby With a Dixie Melody'; 'I'll Say She Does'; California, Here I Come'; 'Four Walls'; 'Me And My Shadow'; Back In Your Own Backyard'; 'Auld Lang Syne'; 'From Monday On'; 'Every Little Movement'; and 'Vesti La Giubba'. Among Al's renderings were 'Sonny Boy', sung no less than three times, and 'Golden Gate', performed in cabaret style rather than sung straight through; Al went through a peripatetic routine, running round the night club floor joking and ad-libbing, and only sporadically breaking in on the melody to add a few lyrics.

1929

AL JOLSON as Joe Lane in

SAY IT WITH SONGS

The Players
Davey Lee (Little Pal), Marion Nixon (Katherine Lane), Fred Kohler (Joe's cellmate), Holmes Herbert (Dr Robert Merrill), Kenneth Thomson (Arthur Phillips).

Warner Bros. – Vitaphone. Directed by Lloyd Bacon. Screenplay by Daryl F. Zanuck, Harvey Gates, Joseph Jackson. Opened 6 August 1929 at the Warner Theatre, New York. Ten reels.

Say It With Songs started life with the tentative title *Little Pal*, taken from one of the songs which Al sang and which he had helped to write. The film included a number of songs which Al not only sang but had also co-authored. These were: 'I'm Ka-razy For You'; 'Back In Your Own Backyard'; 'Used To You'; 'Little Pal'; 'I'm In Seventh Heaven'; 'Why Can't You?'; and 'One Sweet Kiss'. The film was also interesting for the radio-spoofing sequence with which it opened. The supporting cast sang excerpts from 'Il Bacio', 'If I Knew I'd Find You' and 'On the Beach at Waikiki' in this opening scene.

1930

AL JOLSON as Al Fuller in

MAMMY

The Players
Lois Moran (Nora Meadows), Louise Dresser (Al's Mammy), Lowell Sherman (Westy), Noah Beery (Tonopaw Red), Hobart Bosworth (Mr Meadows), Tully Marshall (Slats), Mitchell Lewis (Tambo), Lee Moran (Flat Feet), Jack Curtis (The Sheriff), Stanley Fields (Pig Eyes), Ray Cooke (Props).

Warner Bros. – Vitaphone. Directed by Michael Curtiz. Screenplay by Gordon Rigby and Joseph Jackson. Story and new songs by Irving Berlin. Opened 26 March 1930 at the Warner Theatre, New York. Eight reels.

Named for one of his most famous songs and featuring him in his best known and most characteristic role, that of blackfaced minstrel, *Mammy* gave the movie-going public what Al's stage audiences had been treated to for years. In the course of this celluloid spectacular, Al sang the following songs: 'Knights Of The Road'; 'Let Me Sing And I'm Happy'; 'Who Paid The Rent For Mrs Rip Van Winkle'; 'Yes! We Have No Bananas' – first introduced by Eddie Cantor in 1923, Irving Berlin composed a special parody arrangement of the song for Al to sing in the film; 'My Mammy'; '(Across The Breakfast Table) Looking At You', sung as a romantic ballad in one scene and then as a drunken parody in the scene directly following; 'Why Do They All Take The Night Boat To Albany?'; 'The Call Of the South'; and 'To My Mammy'. Al also sang excerpts from a number of songs in the drunk scene and was accompanied at various points by the Minstrel Quartet or the entire Minstrel Chorus.

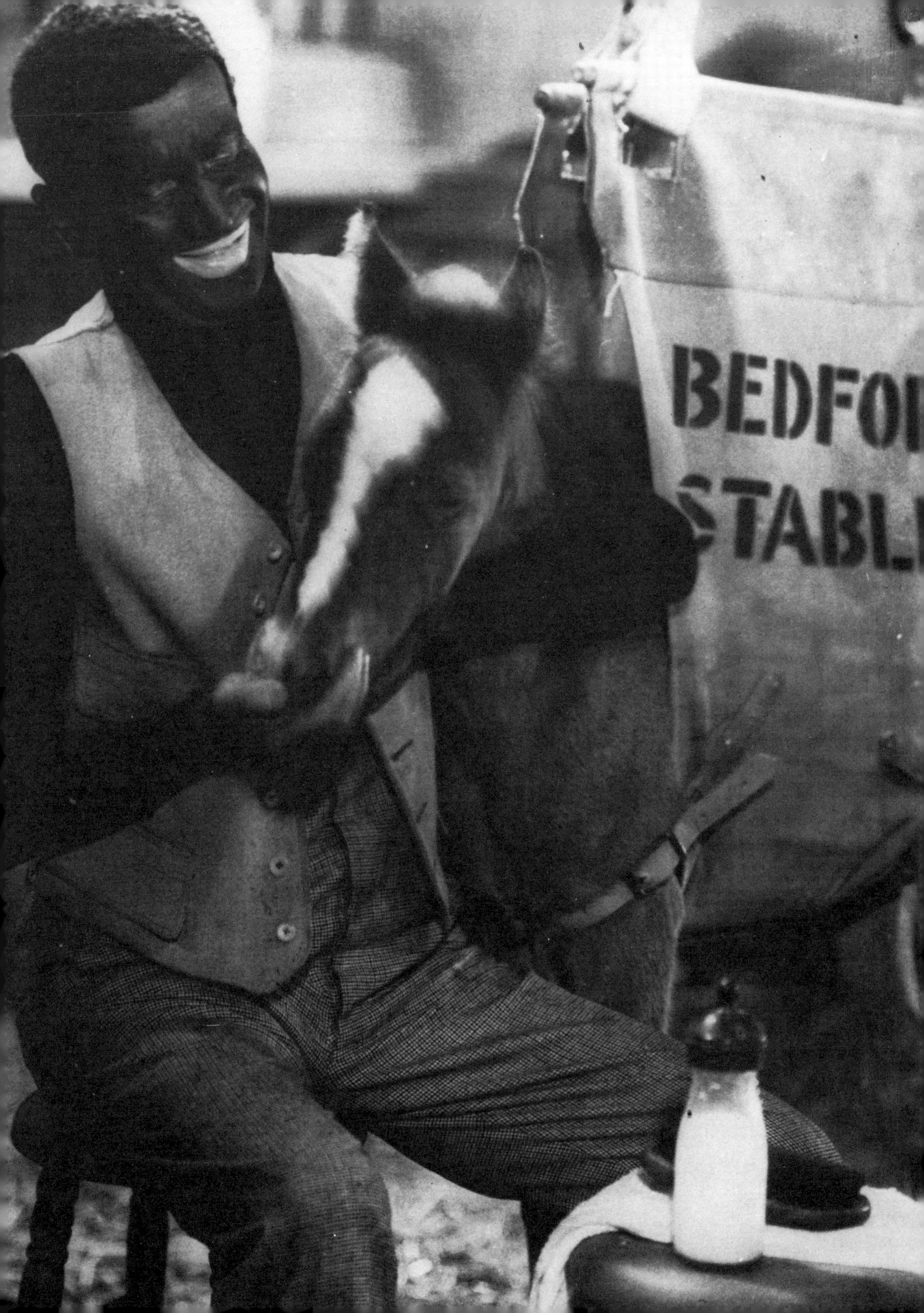
BEDFO
STABL

1930

AL JOLSON as Gus in:

BIG BOY

The Players
Claudia Dell (Annabelle Bedford), Louise Closser Hale (Mrs Bedford), Lloyd Hughes (Jack Bedford), Eddie Phillips (Coley Reed), Lew Harvey (Doc Wilbur), Franklyn A. Batie (Jim), John Harrow (Joe).

Warner Bros – Vitaphone. Directed by Alan Crosland. Screenplay by William J. Wells, Perry Vekroff, Rex Taylor: based upon the musical stage show by Harold Atteridge. Opened 11 September 1930 at the Winter Garden, New York. Nine reels.

This story of the jockey who wins the big race against all the odds shows Al playing more than one role, and undergoing a change of colour and a change of heart in the process. He plays the negro jockey Gus, but also appears blackface in another sequence which flashes back to show him as Gus's grandfather. He then comes on in the final scene – in white-face – threatening to sing 'Sonny Boy'. The audience starts to walk out on him, he withdraws the 'threat', they are restored to their seats and he sings the final selection of songs as Al Jolson. His real-life audience in the cinema saw him sing: 'Hooray For Baby And Me'; 'A Little Sunshine'; 'Liza Lee'; 'Tomorrow Is Another Day'; 'What Will I Do Without You'; and heard 'Down South' and 'The Handicap March' as background music.

Al, as Gus, in *Big Boy* (1930) raises Big Boy for a gallop that will bring victory in the Kentucky Derby.

1933

AL JOLSON as Bumper in:

HALLELUJAH, I'M A BUM

The Players
Madge Evans (June Marcher), Frank Morgan (Mayor Hastings), Harry Langdon (Egghead), Chester Conklin (Sunday), Tyler Brook (Mayor's Secretary,) Tammany Young (Orlando), Bert Roach (John), Victor Potel (The General), Edgar Connor (Acorn), Dorothea Wolbert (Apple Mary), Louise Carver (Ma Sunday), Lorenz Hart (Bank Teller), Richard Rodgers (Assistant Photographer).

United Artists. Directed by Harry d'Abbadie d'Arrast, replaced by Chester Erskin, replaced by Lewis Milestone. Screenplay by S. N. Behrman, from a story by Ben Hecht. Camera: Lucian Andriot. Opened 8 February 1933 at the Rivoli Theatre, New York. Nine reels.

This film was Al's only outing under United Artists' banner, which was just as well for them. Al had put his signature to a contract – drawn up in pencil on a paper bag – which bound Al to make four pictures for the company, and the company to give him half a million dollars for each of them. Al released Joe Schenk from this agreement and saved United Artists from bankruptcy, but went ahead with *Hallelujah, I'm a Bum*, in the distinguished but abrasive company of songwriters Rodgers and Hart. The film was a chequered creation, going into the can by fits and starts. Roland Young, the original Mayor Hastings, fell ill as shooting was almost complete, and the film, then called *Happy Go Lucky*, had to be remade with Frank Morgan in this key role. As well as these changes in cast and title, the film suffered three changes of director. Niceties of idiom also demanded that certain sequences be recorded or shot twice: English-speaking countries of British expression did not see the same film as American audiences and the distributor's delicate sense of tact also resulted in the title being changed to *Hallelujah, I'm a Tramp* for these overseas audiences. Since 1937, when it was reissued by Atlantic Pictures, the picture has gone under further aliases: *The Heart of New York* and, unauthorized both of them, *The New Yorker* and, in England, *Lazy Bones*.

From this celluloid tangle, we can, however, isolate the songs on the *Hallelujah, I'm a Bum* score sheet. These were part of a larger musical score which was dominated by 'rhythmic dialogue', in which Jolson and the rest of the cast participated for half the film's running time. These conversations, set to music by Richard Rodgers, and to rhyme by Lorenz Hart, were an artistic triumph, but, apparently, not to the public taste. Conventional songs which Al and the cast performed were: 'I Gotta Get Back To New York'; 'My Pal Bumper'; 'Hallelujah I'm A Bum'; 'Laying The Cornerstone'; 'Sleeping Beauty'; 'Dear June'; 'Bumper Found A Grand'; 'What Do You Want With Money'; 'Hallelujah, I'm A Bum', a second version; 'Kangaroo Court'; 'I'll Do It Again'; and 'You Are Too Beautiful' – a serenade sung by Al to Madge Evans as he dances with her – and the precedent for this kind of romancing on the move, since seen in scores of film musicals.

'You're right, your Honour' – a prudent admission from Al to Frank Morgan, playing Mayor Hastings, in *Hallelujah, I'm a Bum* (1933).

1934

AL JOLSON as Al Wonder in:

WONDER BAR

The Players
Kay Francis (Liane Renaud), Dolores Del Rio (Inez), Ricardo Cortez (Harry), Dick Powell (Tommy), Himself (Hal LeRoy), Guy Gibbee (Mr Simpson), Ruth Donnelly (Mrs Simpson), Hugh Herbert (Mr Pratt), Louise Fazenda (Mrs Pratt), Fifi D'Orsay (Mitzi), Merna Kennedy (Claire), Robert Barrat (Captain von Ferring).

Warner Bros – First National. Directed by Lloyd Bacon. Screenplay by Earl Baldwin, based upon the musical comedy by Geza Herczeg, Karl Farkas, and Robert Katscher. Production numbers staged by Busby Berkeley. Opened 28 February 1934 at the Strand Theatre, New York. Ten reels.

Wonder Bar was, like *Big Boy*, a chance for screen audiences to see a show which Al had already given on stage. However, the screen, which had formerly been a vehicle for his massive talents, rather seemed to take him over in this picture. Al is no longer in the driving seat all the time and gets swamped in some scenes of *Wonder Bar* by the galaxy of other stars and the sumptuousness of the Busby Berkeley approach. But, though the audience may have seen less of Jolson than they were used to seeing, his performance was nevertheless spectacularly polished and included a show-stealing final scene, in which he sang 'Goin' To Heaven On A Mule'. His other songs were 'Vive La France' and a brilliant rendering – in the original – of a Russian gypsy song, 'Dark Eyes'.

1935

AL JOLSON as Al Howard and RUBY KEELER as Dorothy Wayne in:

GO INTO YOUR DANCE

The Players
Glenda Farrel (Sadie Howard), Helen Morgan (Luana Bell), Benny Rubin (Dancer), Barton M. Lane (The Duke), Sharon Lynne (Blonde), Patsy Kelly (Irma), Phil Regan (Eddie Rio), Gordon Westcott (Fred), William Davidson (McGee), Joyce Compton (Show Girl), Akim Tamiroff (Mexican), Joseph Cregan (Jackson), Arthur Treacher (Englishman), Ward Bond (Jealous Husband), Themselves (Dubin & Warren).

Warner Bros – First National. Directed by Archie L. Mayo. Screenplay by Earl Baldwin, from the novel by Bradford Ropes. Opened 2 May 1935 at the Capitol Theatre, New York. Ten reels.

This was Al's first film with Ruby Keeler, his wife at that time, whose career he had worked so hard to build in this fallow period of his own life. *Go Into Your Dance* was a great success largely because the married couple made a team that caught the public's imagination, and its adulation was certainly as much for Ruby as it was for Al. Typically, the biggest hit in the film was the number 'About A Quarter To Nine', which Al, in full evening dress, sings to the flowingly robed Ruby. Al also sang: 'Celito Lindo'; 'Mammy I'll Sing To You'; 'Old Folks At Home'; 'Casino De Paree'; 'She's A Latin From Manhattan'; and a few lines of 'Go Into Your Dance'. Ruby contributed 'A Good Old-fashioned Cocktail', to which she and the chorus girls also tap-danced.

1936

AL JOLSON as Al Jackson in:

THE SINGING KID

The Players
Allen Jenkins (Joe Eddy), Lyle Talbot (Bob Carey), Frank Mitchell (Dope), William Davidson (Barney Hammond), Edward Keane (Potter), Sybil Jason (Sybil Haines), Tom Manning (Doorman), Wini Shaw (Singer), Edward Everett Horton (Davenport Rogers), Beverly Roberts (Ruth Haines), Jack Durant (Babe), Joseph King (Dr May), Joseph Crehan (Fulton), Claire Dodd (Dana Lawrence), Kay Hughes (Mary Lou), John Hale (Dr Brown), Hattie M. Daniel (Maid); with The Four Yacht Boys and Cab Calloway and his Band.

The Singing Kid provided Al with all the excuse he needed to hold the centre of the stage in a film which, as its title implies, was just made for him. Directly following the title credits and preceding the film proper, a film montage featured Al in a flashback medley of seven outstanding Jolson hits. Against an ever-shifting backdrop and through numerous costume changes, Al sang a few bars from the following songs: 'My Mammy'; 'Swanee'; 'Rockabye Your Baby With A Dixie Melody'; 'California Here I Come'; 'April Showers'; 'About A Quarter To Nine'; and 'Sonny Boy'. All except the last two he sang in blackface. The film itself featured 'I Love To Sing-a', which appeared in three different guises. The first version was sung by Al with some help from Cab Calloway, the second, a much more elaborate performance, with Al's 'My Mammy' counterpointing the Yacht Club Boys' lyrical invitations to try something more modern. The third version featured Al and, briefly, Beverley Roberts. As was common at the time, Al was animated for his pains; a 1937 cartoon with the same title as the song featured 'Owl Jolson' doing yet another variation on the same theme. Other songs which he sang – in the film – with occasional help from the rest of the cast were: 'Who's The Swingest Man in Town'; 'Save Me Sister'; 'Here's Looking At You'; 'You're The Cure For What Ails Me'; and an excerpt from 'All Of Me'.

Mr and Mrs Al Jolson caught in a tender moment during *Go Into Your Dance* (1935), the first film that Al and Ruby Keeler made together.

AL JOLSON as Ted Cotter, TYRONE POWER as Bart Clinton, ALICE FAYE as Rose Sargent in:

ROSE OF WASHINGTON SQUARE

The Players
William Frawley (Harry Long), Joyce Compton (Peggy), Hobart Cavanaugh (Whitey Boone), Moroni Olsen (Buck Russell), E. E. Clive (Barouche Driver), Louis Prima (Band-leader), Charles Wilson (Mike Cavanaugh), Hal Dawson & Paul Burns (Chumps), Ben Walden (Tony), Horace M. Mahon (Irving), Paul Stanton (District Attorney), Winifred Harris (Mrs Russell), John Hamilton (Judge), Adrian Morris (Jim), Charles Lane (Sam Kress), Harry Hayden (Dexter), Maurice Cass (Mr Mok).

20th Century Fox. Directed by Gregory Ratoff. Produced by Daryl F. Zanuck. Screenplay by Nunnally Johnson, from a story by John Larkin and Jerry Horwin. Opened 5 May 1939 at the Roxy Theatre, New York. Eight reels.

In *Rose of Washington Square,* Al had to be content with third billing behind two young stars more in keeping with contemporary taste. However, no other changes in circumstance were visible after the credits had passed. Al was in the film just to play himself, and, for the purposes of the plot, to provide friendship for Alice Faye, a player on the same vaudeville bill, plus, as the film progresses, some avuncular advice for her young ears. Far more important than such character acting, good as it turned out to be, was the opportunity for Al to take the audience by the scruff of its neck with his vibrant stage act. The screenplay may have named the vaudeville singer Ted Cotter, but the cast could have been forgiven if they kept forgetting that. The trouper who sang: 'Pretty Baby'; 'Rockabye Your Baby With A Dixie Melody'; 'Toot, Toot, Tootsie Goo'bye'; 'California, Here I Come'; 'April Showers'; and 'My Mammy' – could have been no one else but Jolson.

Al and Alice Faye go through the same motions of meeting the press in *Rose of Washington Square* that they went through almost daily in real life.

1939

ALICE FAYE as Molly Adair and DON AMECHE as Michael Linnett Connors in:

HOLLYWOOD CAVALCADE

The Players
J. Edward Bromberg (Dave Spingold), Alan Curtis (Nicky Hayden), Stuart Irwin (Pete Tinney), Jed Prouty (Chief of Police), Himself (Buster Keaton), Donald Meek (Lyle P. Stout), George Givot (Englishman), Eddie Collins, Hank Mann, Heinie Conklin, James Finlayson (Keystone Kops), Chick Chandler (Assistant Director), Robert Lowery (Henry Potter), Russell Hicks (Roberts), Ben Walden (Agent), Willie Fung (Valet), Paul Stanton (Wilson), Ben Turpin (Bartender), Chester Conklin (Sheriff), Himself (Mack Sennett), Marjorie Beebe (Telephone Operator), Frederick Burton (Thomas), Himself (Lee Duncan), Rin Tin Tin Jr. (Rin Tin Tin), with a special appearance of AL JOLSON.

20th Century Fox. Directed by Irving Cummings. Produced by Daryl F. Zanuck. Screenplay by Ernest Pascal, from a story by Hilary Lynn and Brown Holmes. Opened 13 October 1939 at the Roxy Theatre, New York. Ten reels.

This fictitious love story, interwoven with the factual history of the cinema, gave many prominent film stars the chance to retrace their most famous steps. Alice Faye, sharing a cast list with Buster Keaton, the Keystone Kops and Rin Tin Tin, was not one of those who was going through an old routine, however. This did not prevent her being welcomed in traditional fashion by these old stagers; perhaps the strongest scene in the film shows her being hit in the face by a custard pie. Al Jolson, in stark contrast to these expansive slapstick hijinks, appears only once, in a tiny non-speaking part, encoring the famous synagogue scene from *The Jazz Singer*. In this he sings 'Kol Nidre', in Aramaic, with the backing of a choir.

1939

AL JOLSON as Edwin Palmer Christy, DON AMECHE as Stephen Foster, ANDREA LEEDS as Jane McDowell in:

SWANEE RIVER

The Players
Felix Brossart (Henry Kleber), Chick Chandler (Bones), Russell Hicks (Andrew McDowell), George Reed (Old Black Joe), Richard Clarke (Tom Harper), Diane Fisher (Marion Foster), George Breakstone (Ambrose), Al Herman (Tambo), Charles Two Bridge (Mr Foster), George Meeker (Henry Foster), Leora Roberts (Mrs Foster), Charles Tannen (Morrison Foster), Nella Walker (Mrs McDowell), Harry Hayden (Erwin), Clara Bandick (Mrs Griffin), Esther Dale (Temperance Women), and The Hall Johnson Choir.

20th Century Fox. Directed by Sidney Lanfield. Produced by Daryl F. Zanuck. Screenplay by John Tainter Foote and Philip Dunne, from the life of Stephen Foster. Dances staged by Nick Castle and Geneva Sawyer. Opened 29 December 1939 at the Roxy Theatre, New York. Eight reels.

Swanee River, a rather florid account of the life of song-writer Stephen Foster, gave Al the chance to shine on celluloid once more. In the film, he played E. P. Christie, the great minstrel who with his company presented many of the Foster ballads to the public for the first time. Al turned in one of his finest screen performances; his enthusiasm for real work – after a rather unsuitable interlude as a make-weight – bubbles through his performance. Perhaps the most memorable moment was his singing of 'The Old Folks At Home', but he reached almost as high with 'Oh! Susanna', 'De Camptown Races' and 'My Old Kentucky Home'. The rest of the film, at the very least, reminded the audience how many of the songs that they sang and hummed day by day, came from the pen of Stephen Foster.

1945

AL JOLSON with Oscar Levant, Paul Whiteman, George White, Hazel Scott, Anne Brown, Tom Patricola, John B. Hughes, Elsa Maxwell, The Warner Choral Singers as themselves in:

RHAPSODY IN BLUE

The Players
Robert Alda (George Gershwin), Joan Leslie (Julie Adams), Alexis Smith (Christine Gilbert), Charles Coburn (Max Dreyfus), Julie Blahoe (Lee Gershwin), Herbert Rudley (Ira Gershwin), Albert Basserman (Professor Frank), Morris Carnovsky (Mr Gershwin), Rosemary Decamp (Mrs Gershwin), Eddie Marr (Buddy DeSylva), Oscar Loraine (Ravel), Hugo Kirvhhoffer (Walter Damrosch), Mickey Roth (George Gershwin, as a boy), Darryl Hickman (Ira Gershwin, as a boy), Charles Halton (Mr Kast), Andrew Tombes (Mr Million), Gregory Gollibeff (Mr Katzman), Theodore Von Eltz (Foley), Bill Kennedy (Herbert Stone), Robert Shane (American Man), Johnny Downs (Dancer), Ernest Gulm (Otto Kahn), Martin Noble (Heifetz), Will Wright (Rachmaninoff).

Warner Bros. Directed by Irving Rapper. Produced by Jesse L. Lasky. Screenplay by Howard Koch and Elliot Paul, from the story by Sonya Levien based on the life of George Gershwin. Camera: Morritt Gersted and Ernest Haller. Opened 27 June 1945 at the Hollywood Theatre, New York. Fourteen reels.

Transparent as his performance may have been in most films, Al did not even have to pretend to be anyone but himself in *Rhapsody in Blue*; his was only a cameo part in this biographical picture based on George Gershwin's life. The part was small, but Gershwin was an old friend of Jolson's and it did provide an opportunity to step back in front of the cameras in blackface. Though Al was not fully fit when he was shooting, his singing of 'Swanee' comes across almost as well as when he first introduced it in 1919, in his show, *Sinbad*. Al was to have received $25,000 for his offering but actually appeared free, perhaps as a mark of respect for Gershwin. The film, being shot in World War II, took several years to produce, and Jolson's scene may have been shot and recorded more than once; certainly clips of him from *Rhapsody in Blue* appear in several other movies. *Rhapsody in Blue*, with its galaxy of guest stars, may not have plumbed George Gershwin's character, but his music, which dominates the film, speaks for itself, providing its own lament for what the world missed by the great man's early death.

1946

The voice of AL JOLSON in:

THE JOLSON STORY

with LARRY PARKS as AL JOLSON

The Players
Evelyn Keyes (Julie Benson), William Demarest (Steve Martin), Bill Goodwin (Tom Baron), Ludwig Donath (Cantor Yoelson), Tamara Shayne (Mama Yoelson), John Alexander (Lew Dockstader), Jo Carroll Dennison (Ann Murray), Ernest Cossart (Father McGee), Scotty Beckett (Al Jolson, as a boy), William Forrest (Dick Glenn), Ann Todd (Anne Murray, as a girl), Edwin Maxwell (Oscar Hammerstein I), Emmett Vogan (Jonesy), Eric Wilton (Henry), Will Wright (Movie Heckler), and The Mitchell Boychoir.

Columbia Pictures Corporation. Directed by Alfred E. Green. Produced by Sidney Skolsky. Screenplay by Stephen Longstreet, with additional material by Harry Chandler and Andrew Solt. Camera: Joseph Walker. Dances staged by Jack Cole. Opened 10 October 1946 at the Radio City Music Hall, New York. Fourteen reels.

The Jolson Story was the film that gave both the man and the legend a new lease of life. It also gave a public accustomed to singing microphones an idea of what real entertainers were all about. In the film, Larry Parks, miming to Al's perfectly sung vocals, traces the rise of the World's Greatest Entertainer. From Park's mute larynx, Al conjured the following songs: 'Let Me Sing And I'm Happy; 'When You Were Sweet Sixteen'; 'Ma Blushin' Rose'; I Want A Girl'; 'My Mammy'; 'I'm Sitting On Top Of The World'; 'You Made Me Love You'; 'Toot, Toot, Tootsie Goo'bye'; 'The Spaniard That Blighted My Life'; 'April Showers'; 'California, Here I Come'; 'Liza'; 'There's A Rainbow 'Round My Shoulder'; 'Avalon'; 'About A Quarter To Nine'; 'Anniversary Song'; 'Waiting For The Robert E. Lee'; 'Rockabye Your Baby With A Dixie Melody'; and 'April Showers'. Al also provided the whistling of 'Blue Bell'. A boy vocalist provided the voice for Scotty Beckett, who played Al Jolson as a boy.

So meticulous and critical was Al's tutelage of Larry Parkes, that the actor managed an impressive simulation of Al's characteristic poses and gestures.

On two songs, Al did not need a proxy. 'Let Me Sing And I'm Happy' provided the film with its title song, so no actors were necessary. He also actually appeared later in the film – singing an abbreviated version of 'Swanee'. A succession of long shot shots 'hide' his face from the camera, but there is no mistaking the maestro's eloquence and variety of gesture, even in that short time. As for the rest of the film – if we are deprived of the man's charismatic presence – there is still the unrivalled consolation of his voice.

Ludwig Donath, who played Cantor Yoelson in both *The Jolson Story* and its sequel looked much like the real Cantor Yoelson and also managed to create an uncanny duplication of Moses Yoelson's stern, quizzical expression.

1949

The Voice of AL JOLSON in:

JOLSON SINGS AGAIN

with LARRY PARKS as AL JOLSON

The Players
Barbara Hale (Ellen Clark), William Demarest (Steve Martin), Ludwig Donath (Cantor Yoelson), Bill Goodwin (Tom Baron), Myron M. Cormack (Ralph Bryant), Tamara Shayne (Mama Yoelson), Eric Wilton (Henry), Robert Emmett Keane (Charlie).

Columbia Pictures Corporation. Directed by Henry Levin. Produced by Sidney Buchman from his own screenplay. Camera: William Syder. Opened 17 August 1949 at Loew's State, New York. Ten reels.

Carrying on where *The Jolson Story* left off, *Jolson Sings Again* tells the rest of Al's tale. The continuity between the two films was handled with an obsessive attention to realism. A clip of Larry Parks 'singing' 'Rockabye Your Baby With A Dixie Melody', taken from the closing scene of the first film, directly follows the credits of *Jolson Sings Again*, preceding the film itself. Towards the end of this film, a complex sequence, using original soundtrack from the first film, re-created the shooting of *The Jolson Story*. Larry Parks plays both himself and Al Jolson in an impressive series of character switches which reconstruct the action on the set of the first film. This display of cinematic self-consciousness is capped by a scene showing *The Jolson Story*'s sneak preview, when the audience were shown clips from that film. In *Jolson Sings Again*, the clips are supported by a discreet voice-over which serves to keep the story of the sequel going.

With the completion of the film biography and a revival of interest in Jolson, radio stations were deluged with plugs for the films and records issued along with them. To this renewed outpouring of Jolson's music, *Jolson Sings Again* contributed the following songs (mimed once again by Larry Parks and sung, of course, by Al himself); 'Is It True What They Say About Dixie?'; 'For Me And My Gal'; 'Back In

This studio panorama from *Jolson Sings Again* summarises the kind of self-conscious reconstruction necessary in the making of show business biographies.